Dunmore East, Co. Waterford

Emmet Tobin

BY HOOK OR BY CROOK

Hook Peninsula, home to the world's oldest working lighthouse, is located on the east side of the entrance to Waterford Harbour. On the other side lies the parish of Crook.

Dunmore East, Co. Waterford

Contents

Dunmore East, Co. Waterford

Dunmore East, Co. Waterford

The Story of Dunmore East

Iron Age people established a promontory fort overlooking the sea at Shanoon (referred to in 1832 as meaning the 'Old Camp' but more likely Canon Power's Sean Uaimh, 'Old Cave') at a point known for centuries as Black Nobb, where the old pilot station now stands, and underneath which a cave runs. Henceforth the place was referred to as Dún Mór, the Great Fort.

Fish was an important part of the people's diet, and for hundreds of years a fishing community lived here.

In 1640, Lord Power of Curraghmore, who owned a large amount of property in the area, built a castle on the cliff overlooking the strand about two hundred metres from St. Andrew's Church. The castle was falling into ruin by the middle of the next century and now just one tower remains.

The old church of Killea (Cill Aodha — Aodh's Church, Aodh is Irish for Hugh) is thought to have been built in the twelfth century and one wall still stands, opposite the Roman Catholic church of The Holy Cross, at the top of Killea Hill.

In Smith's history of Waterford, the village was mentioned as being a fishing port about the year 1745. The fishermen's homes were situated in the Lower Village near the Strand Inn and boats were launched from the slip at Lawlors Beach before the harbour was built. There is mention of a fleet of fifty fishing boats working from Dunmore East in 1776.

In 1812 a decision was made at Westminster to create an entirely new landing point for passengers and mail coming to Ireland from London and southern England. The location selected was Dunmore East and £118,000 was set aside for the erection of a pier there. In 1814 dramatic changes took place when Alexander Nimmo, the Scottish engineer (builder of Limerick's Sarsfield Bridge) commenced work on the new harbour at Dunmore to accommodate the packet station for ships, which carried the Royal Mail between England and Ireland. The work consisted mainly of a massive pier or quay with an elegant lighthouse at the end. Nimmo's original estimate had been £20,000 but at the time of his death in 1832 about £93,000 had been spent and the final cost was £108,000. By then (1837) the harbour had started to silt up, and the arrival of steam meant that the winding river could be negotiated easily, so the packet station was transferred to Waterford.

The great sheltered harbour then constructed meant that Dunmore East was to gradually become an important fishing port. It also then developed into a very popular tourist resort and it is now a favourite port of call for large cruise liners visiting the south east of Ireland.

The Haven Hotel, formerly the Villa Marina, was a holiday home built by the Malcolmsons, who were involved financially in the American Civil War. The Fisherman's Hall in the village was also built by the family for fishermen to mend their nets.

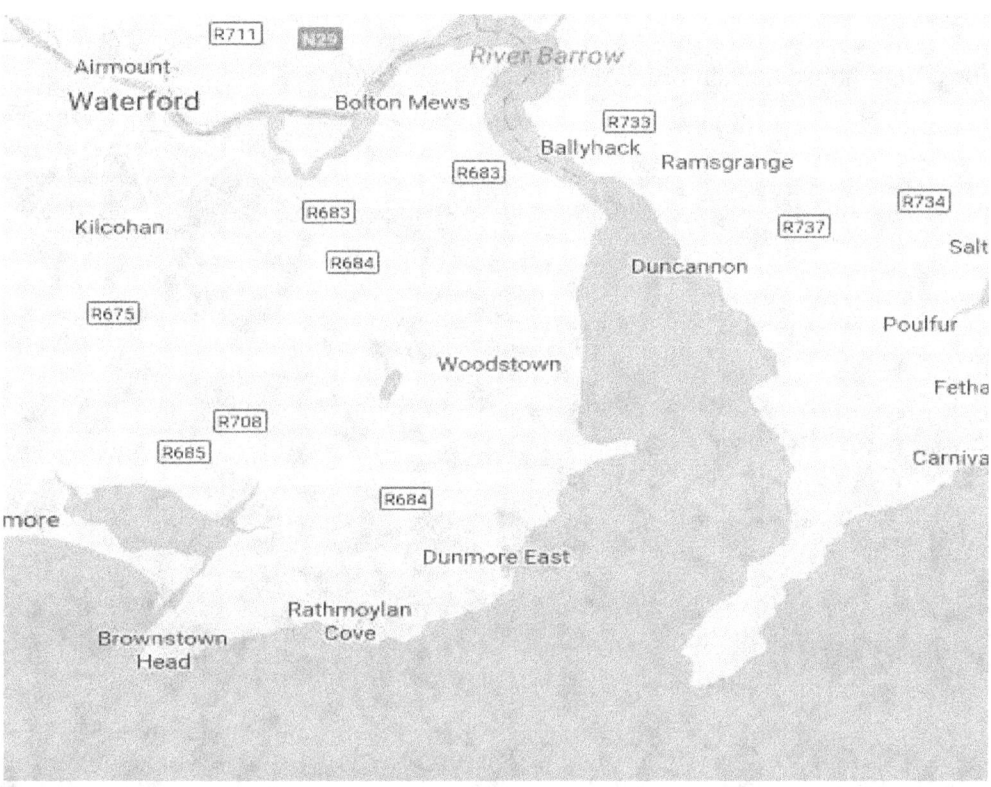

Map of the Dunmore East area and the estuary. The Suir, Nore and Barrow rivers all join the estuary. Collectively, they are known as "The Three Sisters".

Dunmore East, Co. Waterford

Opposite (Top): Hook Lighthouse stands at 35 metres in height. The lighthouse was automated in 1996 and the light keepers departed after almost 800 years.

Opposite (Bottom): Following the coast road out of Dunmore East in the direction of Coxtown and Knockenpadden, the land rises to provide a good vantage point across the harbour entrance (Pictured: Hook Lighthouse).

Below: Hook Lighthouse as pictured from Ladies Cove, Dunmore East.

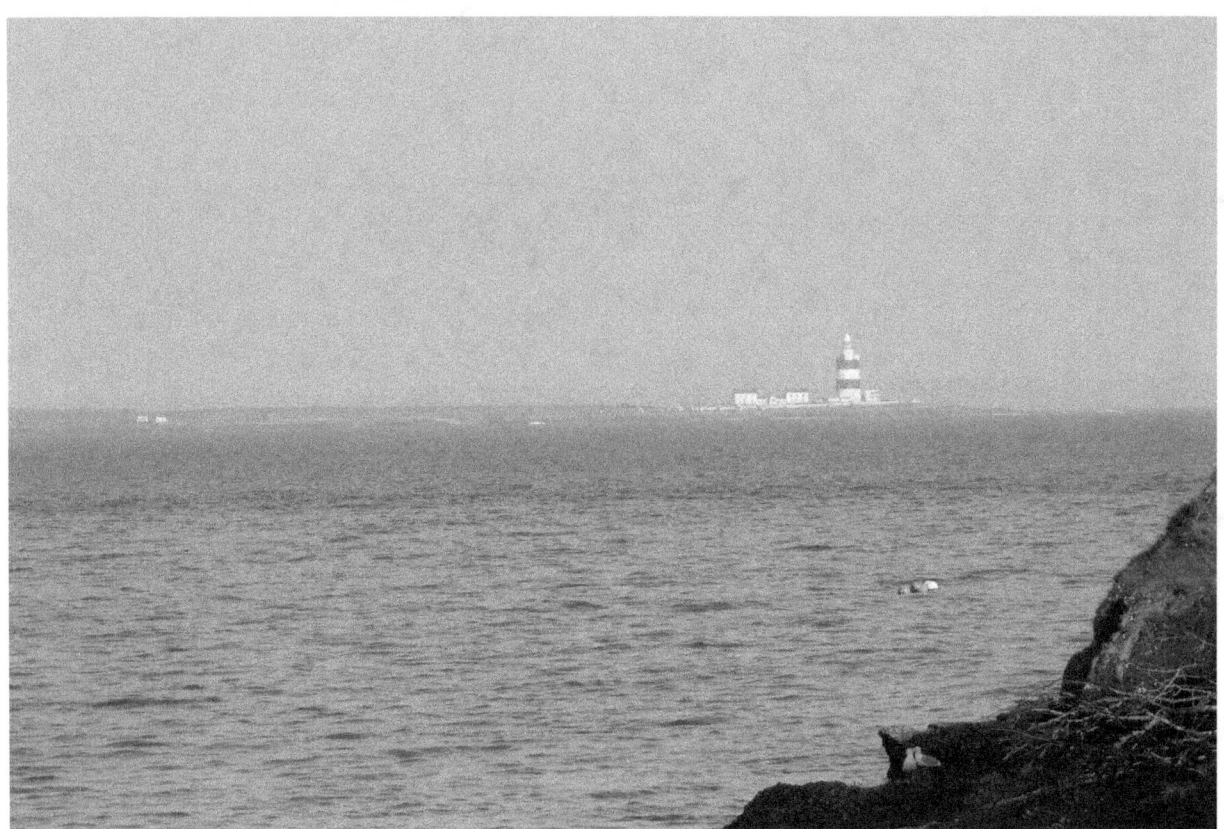

Dunmore East, Co. Waterford

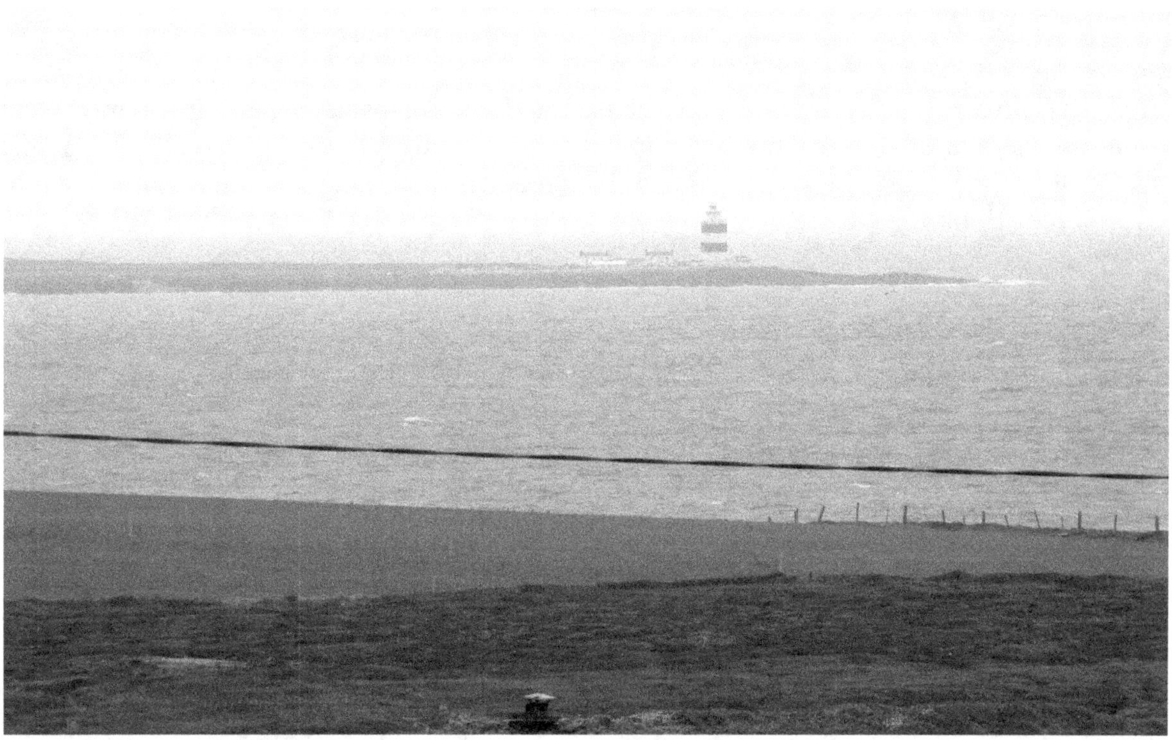

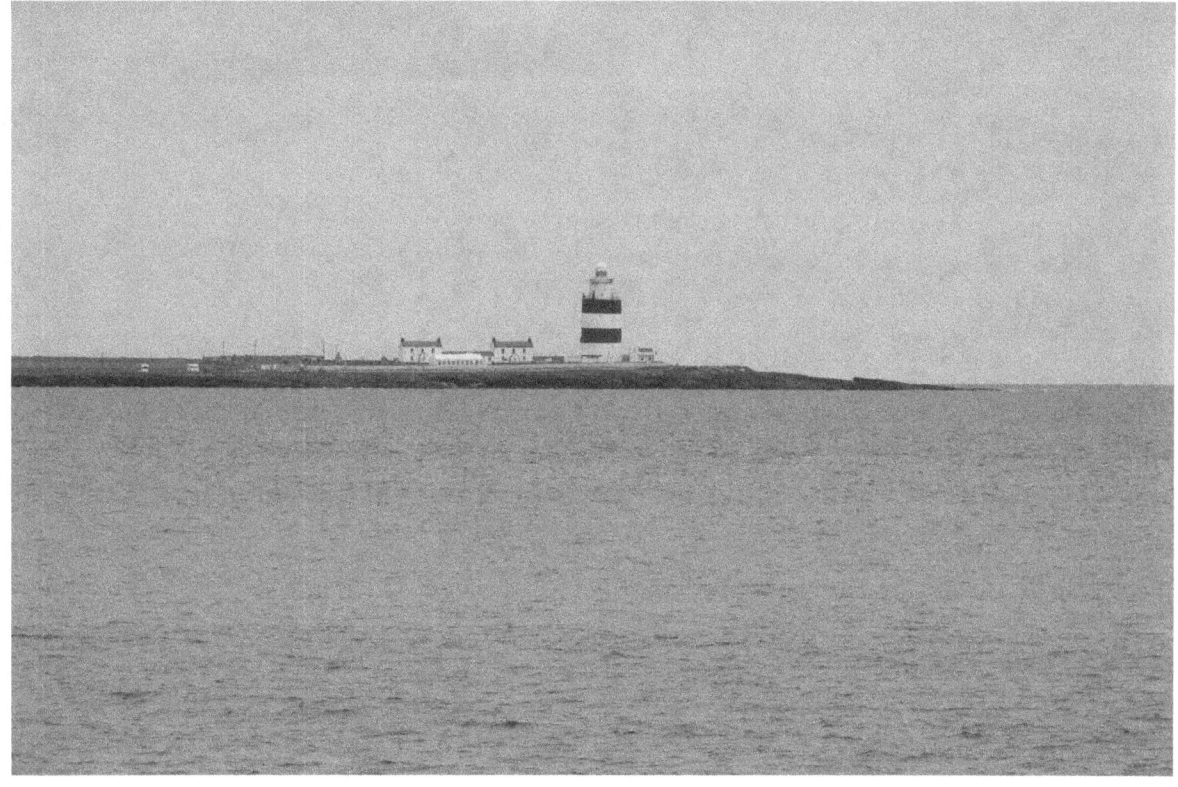

Dunmore East, Co. Waterford

Below: Loftus Hall is a large mansion house on **Hook Peninsula,** located in **County Wexford.** Built on the site of the original Redmond Hall, it is said by locals to have been haunted by the **devil** and the ghost of a young woman. Pictured here from Dunmore East, Loftus Hall lies to the north of Hook Lighthouse.

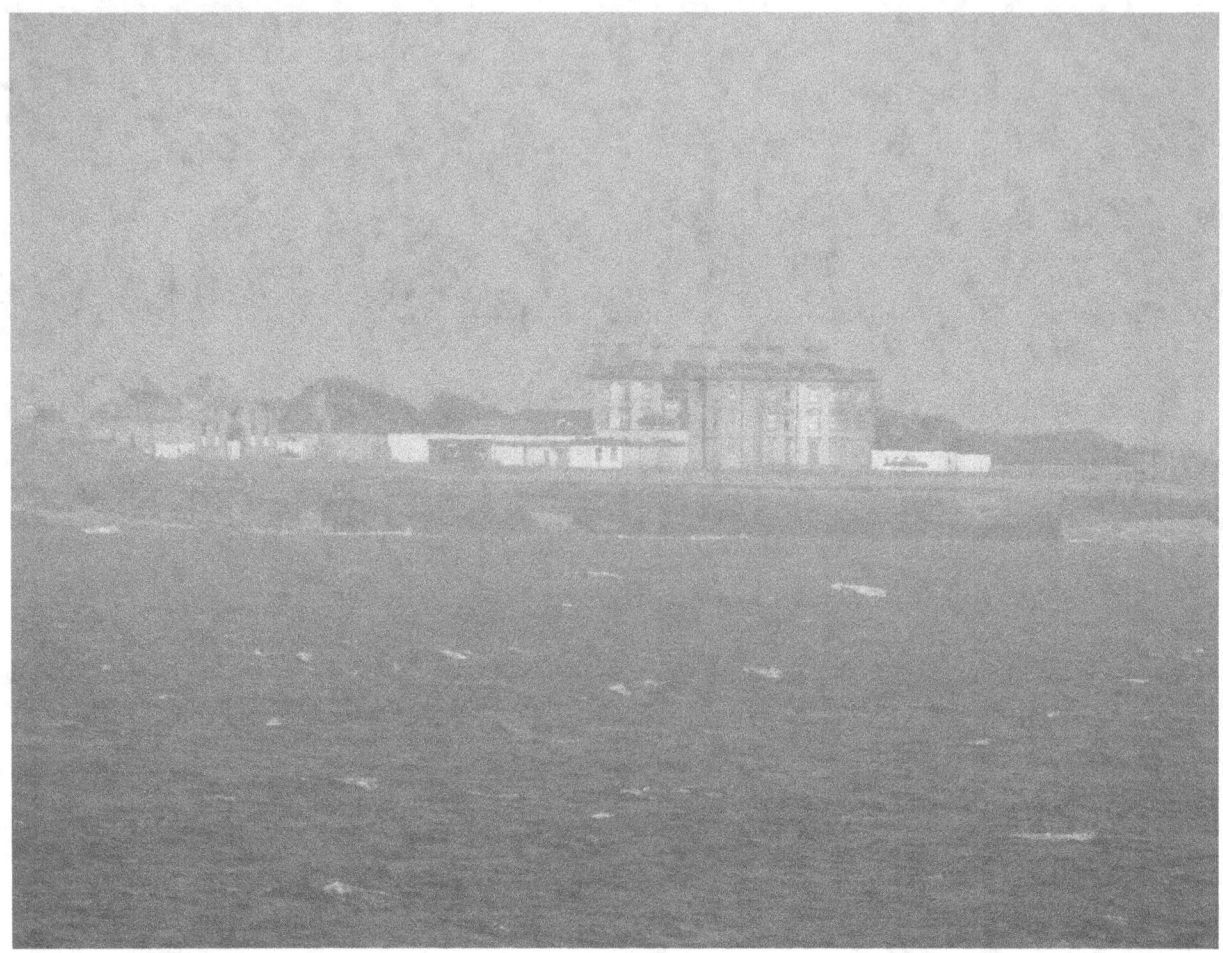

Opposite: Fish shop located in the harbour

Dunmore East, Co. Waterford

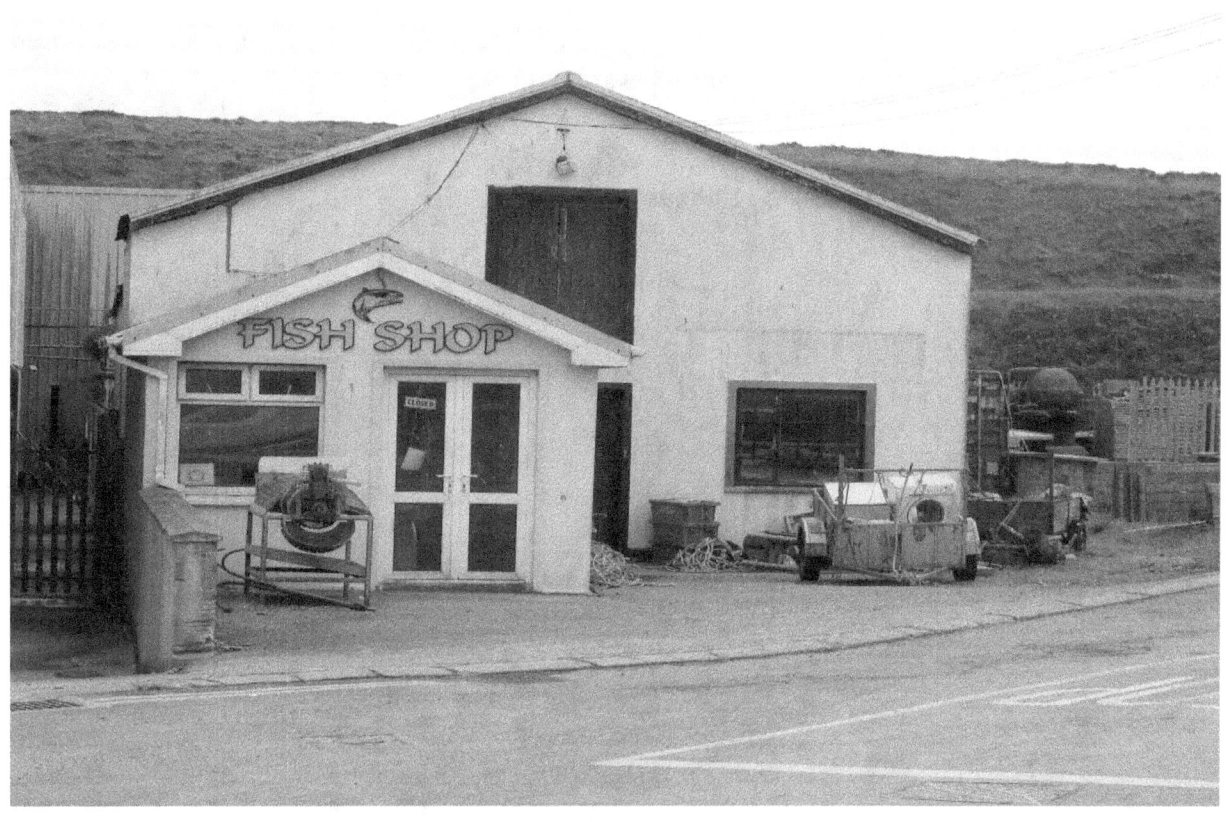

Dunmore East, Co. Waterford

Opposite (Top): With an effective height of 29 metres, the beacon can be seen from a distance of 19 nautical miles. The importance of Dunmore East dates back to 1814. Dunmore was chosen by the Post Office to be the Irish terminal of a new mail packet route from Milford Haven.

Opposite (Bottom): Dunmore East Lighthouse from a distance.

Dunmore East, Co. Waterford

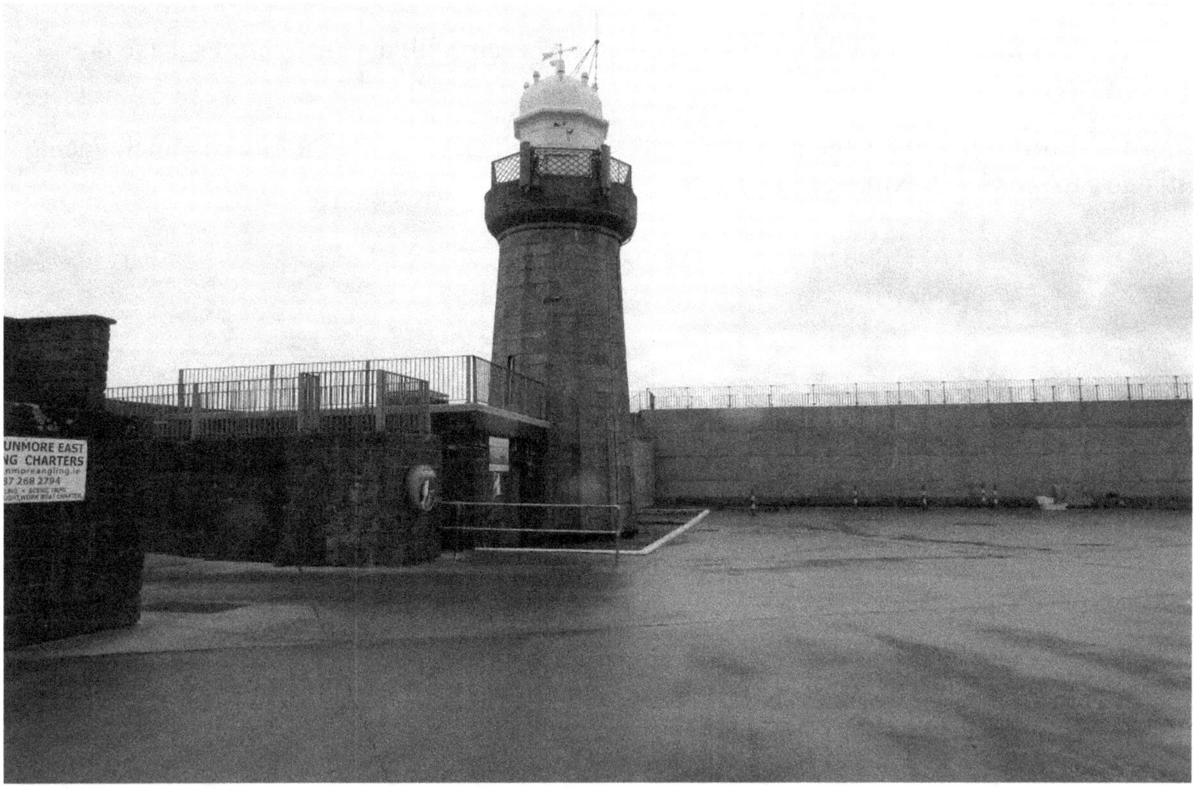

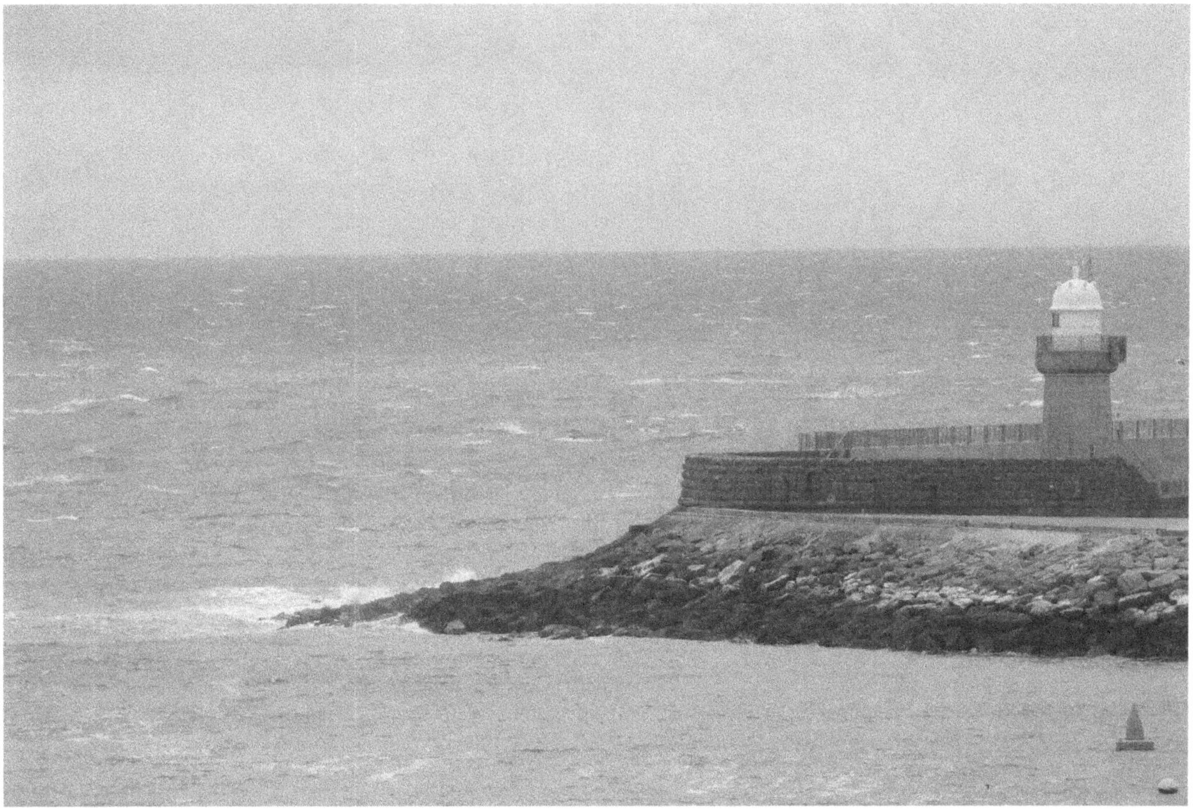

Dunmore East, Co. Waterford

Opposite (Top): Nestled behind the protection of the beach wall, thatched houses make the perfect getaway.

Opposite (Bottom): The People's Park situated in the village opposite the Haven Hotel. Facing east, one can see Co. Wexford across the bay.

Dunmore East, Co. Waterford

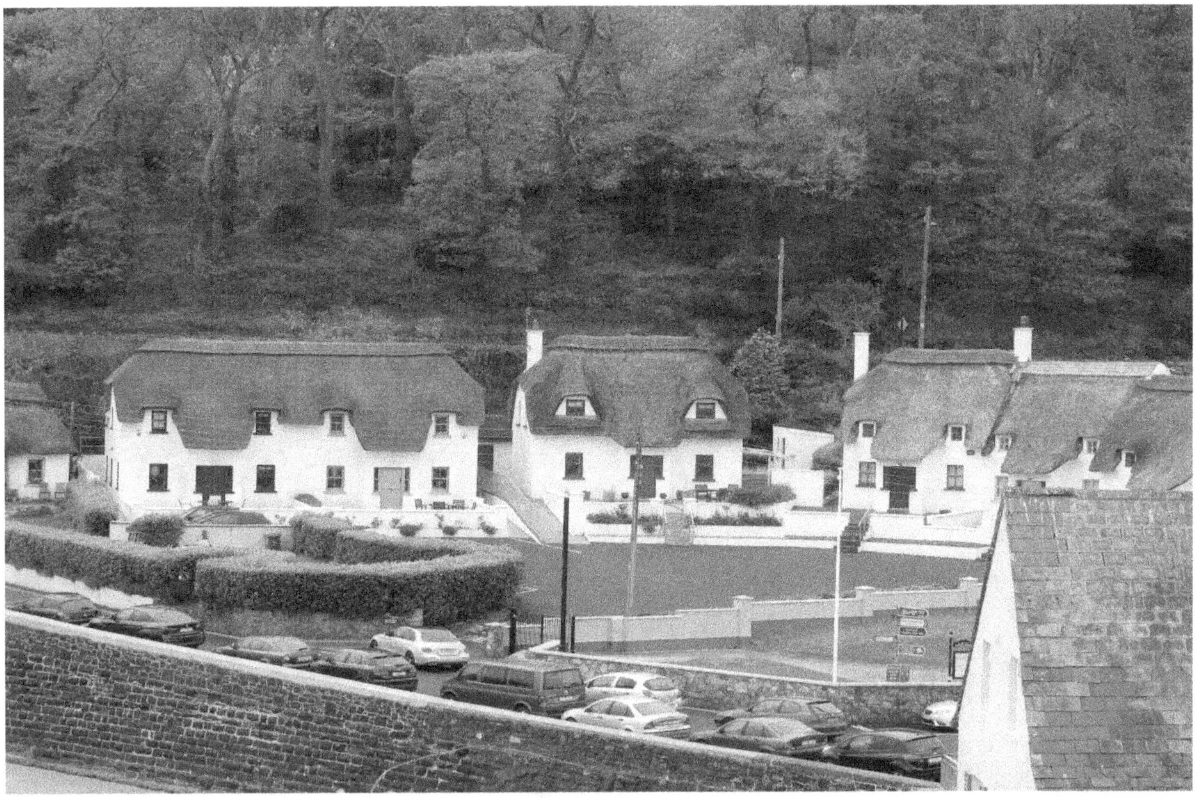

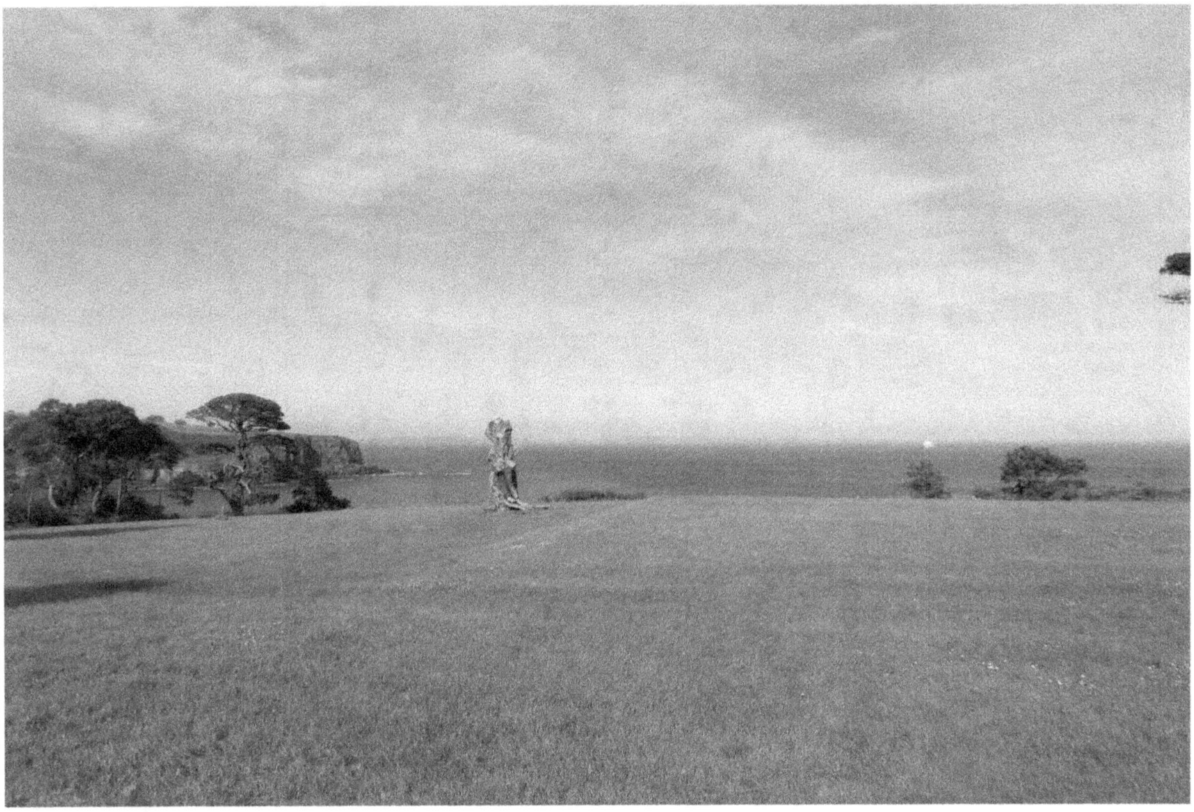

Dunmore East, Co. Waterford

Opposite (Top): A slipway allows entrance to the strand (Lawlors Strand). At high tide, waves make their way up more than halfway.

Opposite (Bottom): Footprints in the sand. Lawlors Strand at low tide.

Dunmore East, Co. Waterford

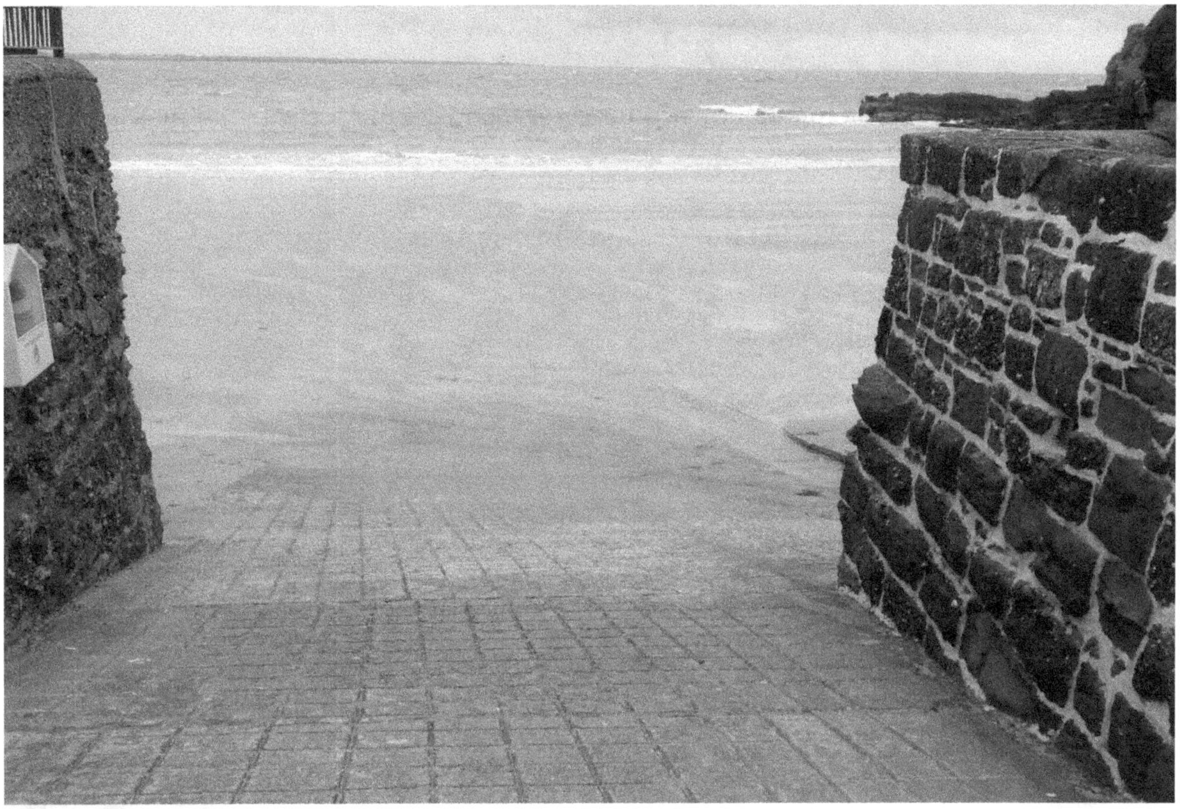

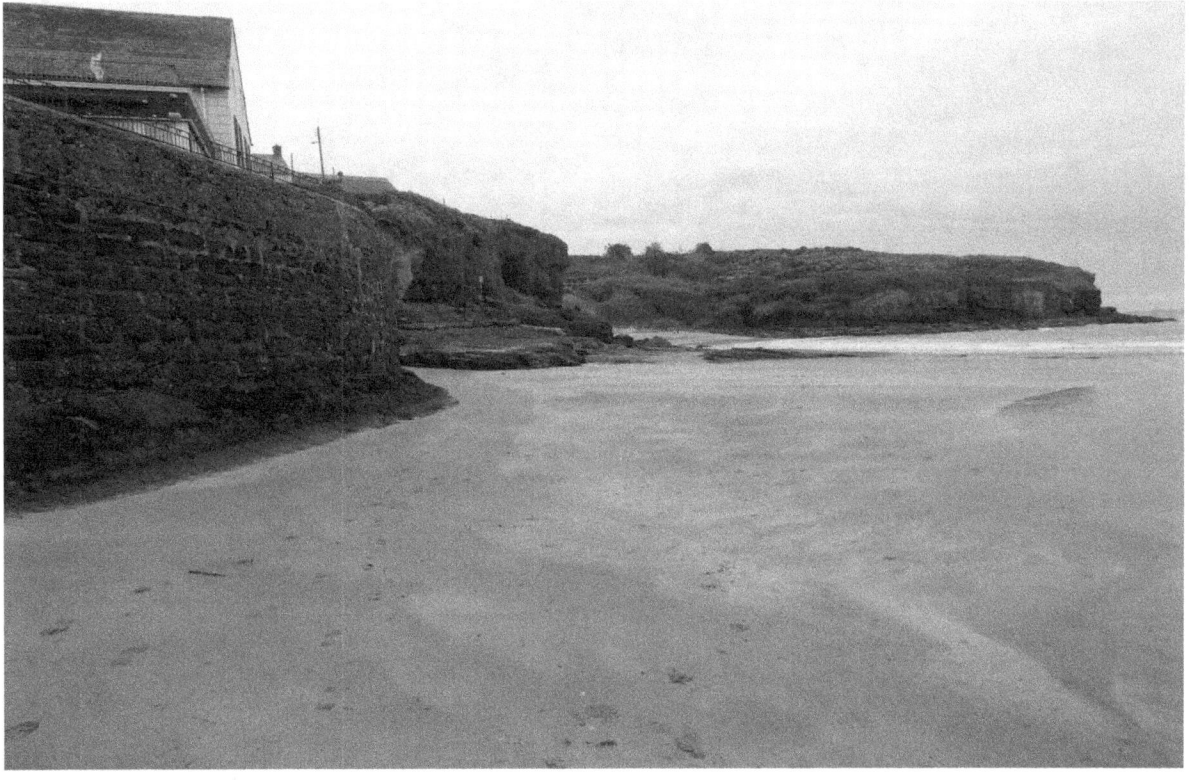

Opposite (Top): The Strand Inn. Renowned for great food with the perfect seafront setting.

Opposite (Bottom): The Strand Inn from a short distance away.

Dunmore East, Co. Waterford

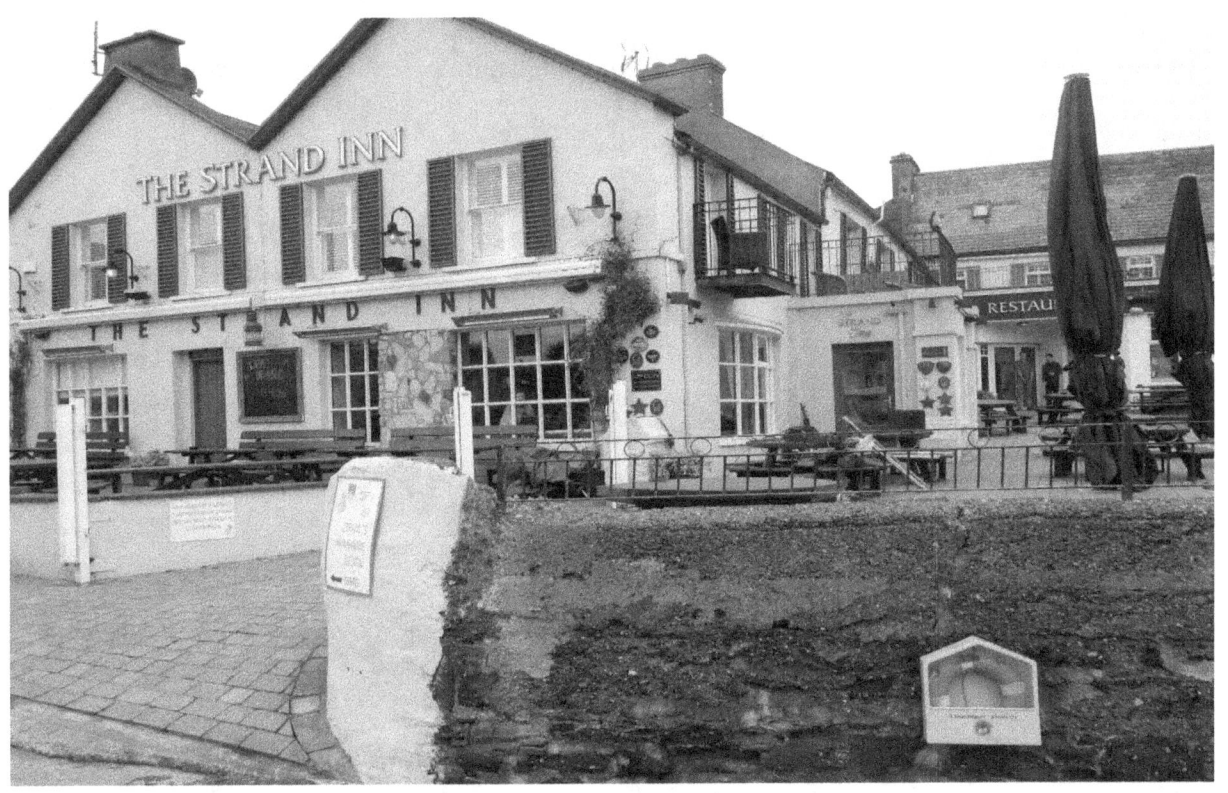

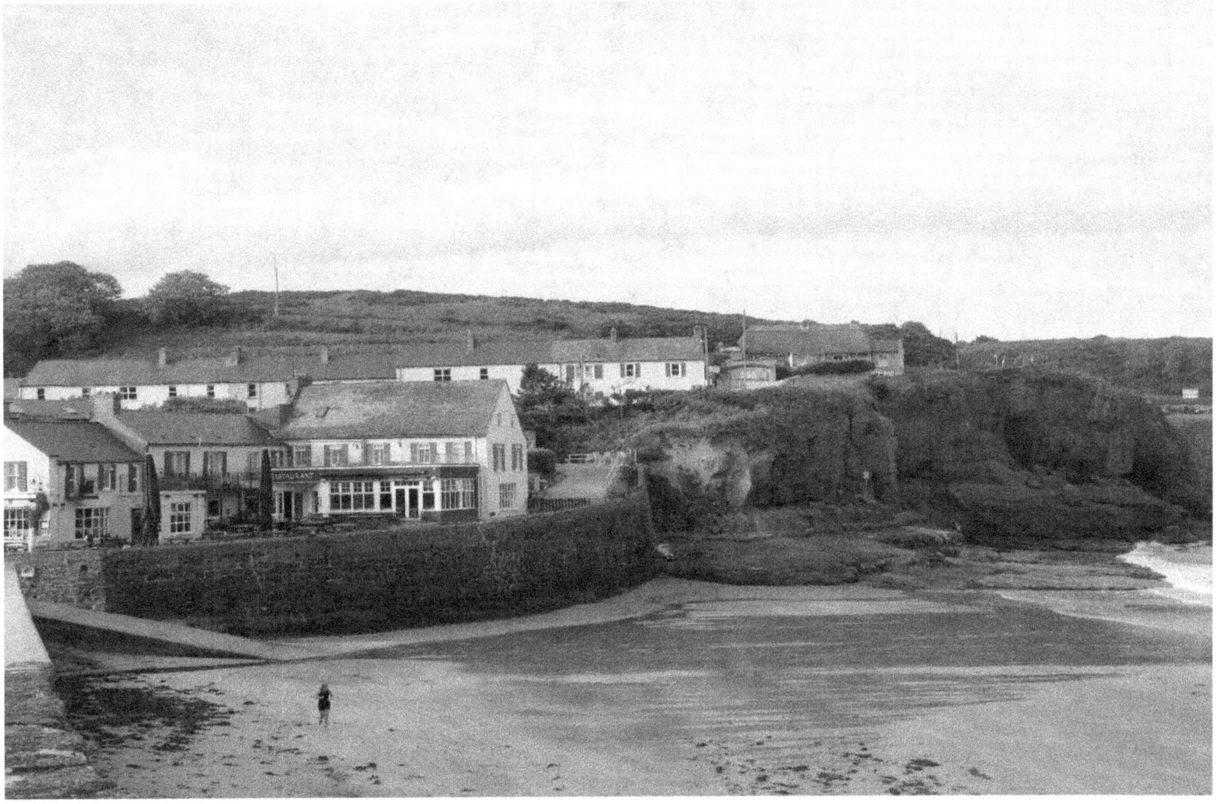

Dunmore East, Co. Waterford

Opposite (Top): Standing sentry on the Harbour wall railing, a young Glaucous Gull, yet to develop its full plumage, poses resolutely. For many years the Harbour wall had no railings in place.

Opposite (Bottom): A busy harbour provides plenty of fish guts for winged wildlife. However, time must be made for preening also.

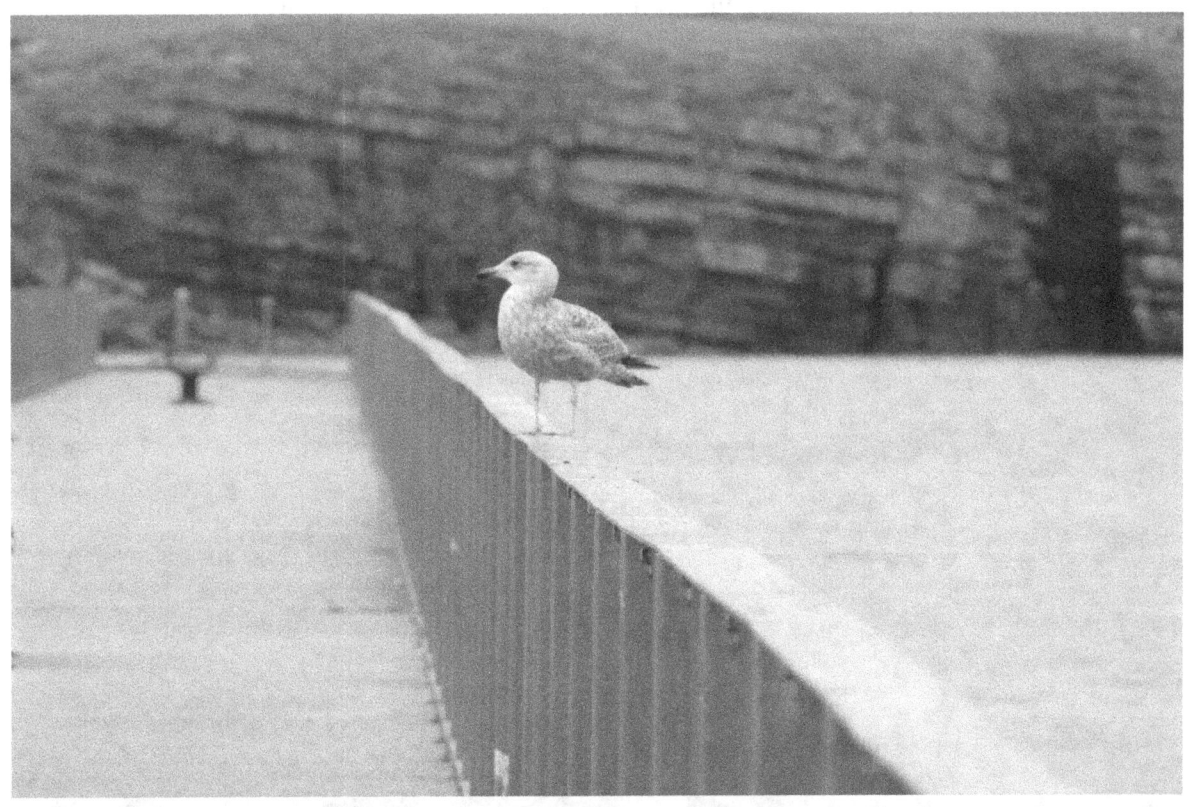

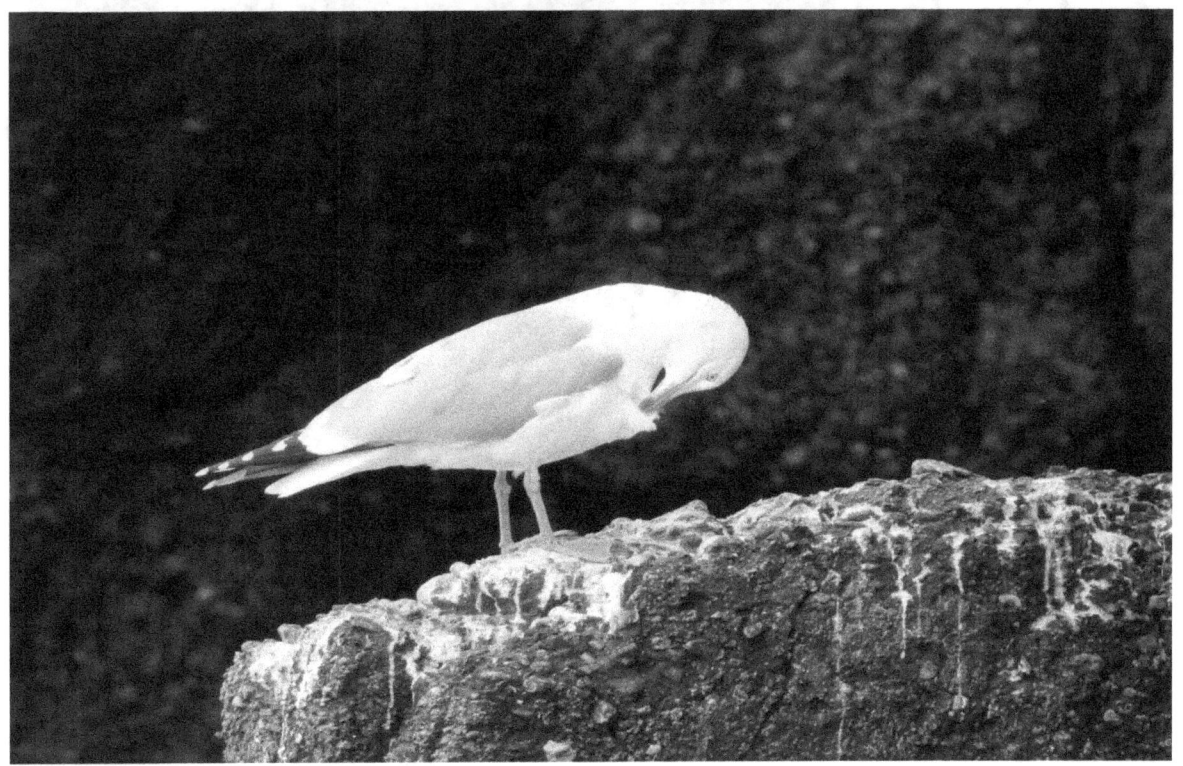

Dunmore East, Co. Waterford

Opposite (Top): Quite the meal. ("It prefers a flesh diet, either recent or ancient, a dead rat, dog or whale is alike acceptable to the corpse eater. T.A. Coward")

Opposite (Bottom): A western yellow-legged gull pictured in the Harbour at Dunmore East.

Below: Beak parted, the sound of the gull travels a long distance.

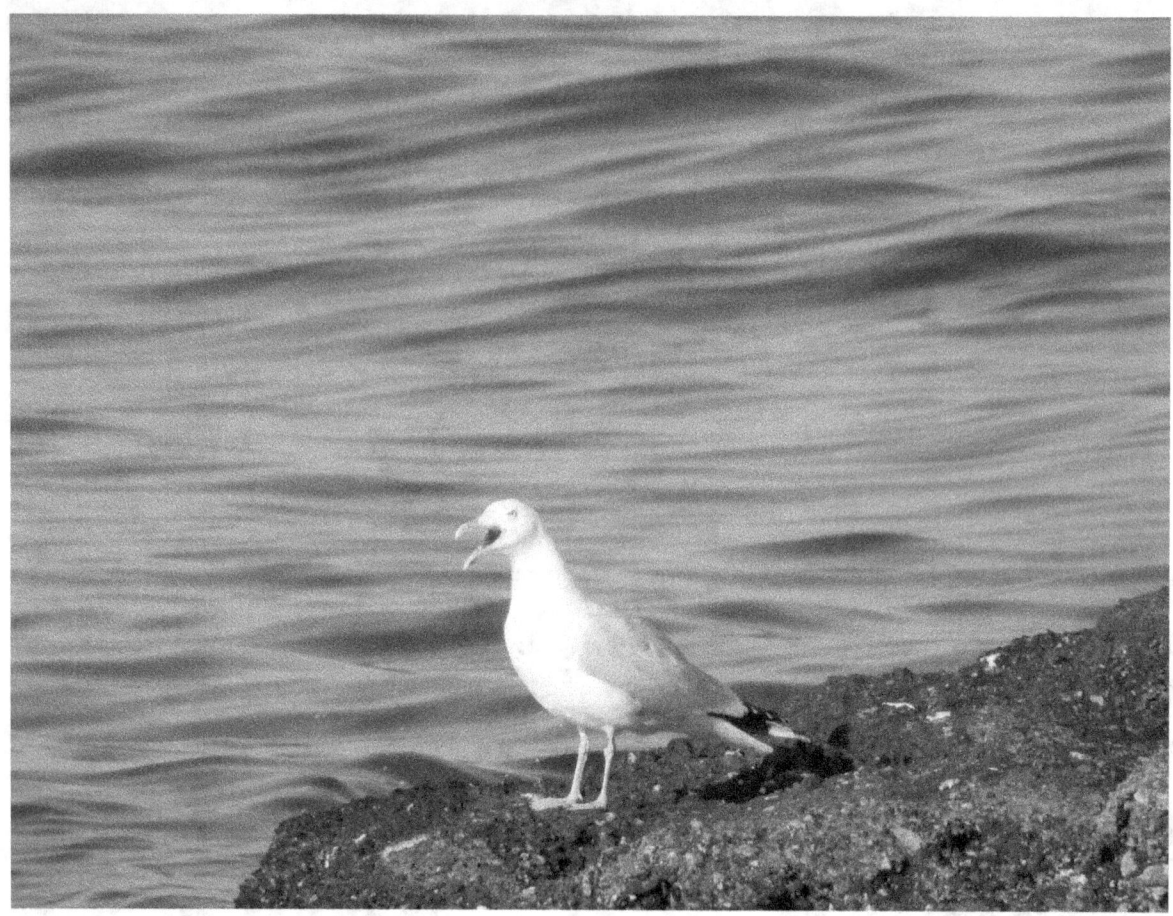

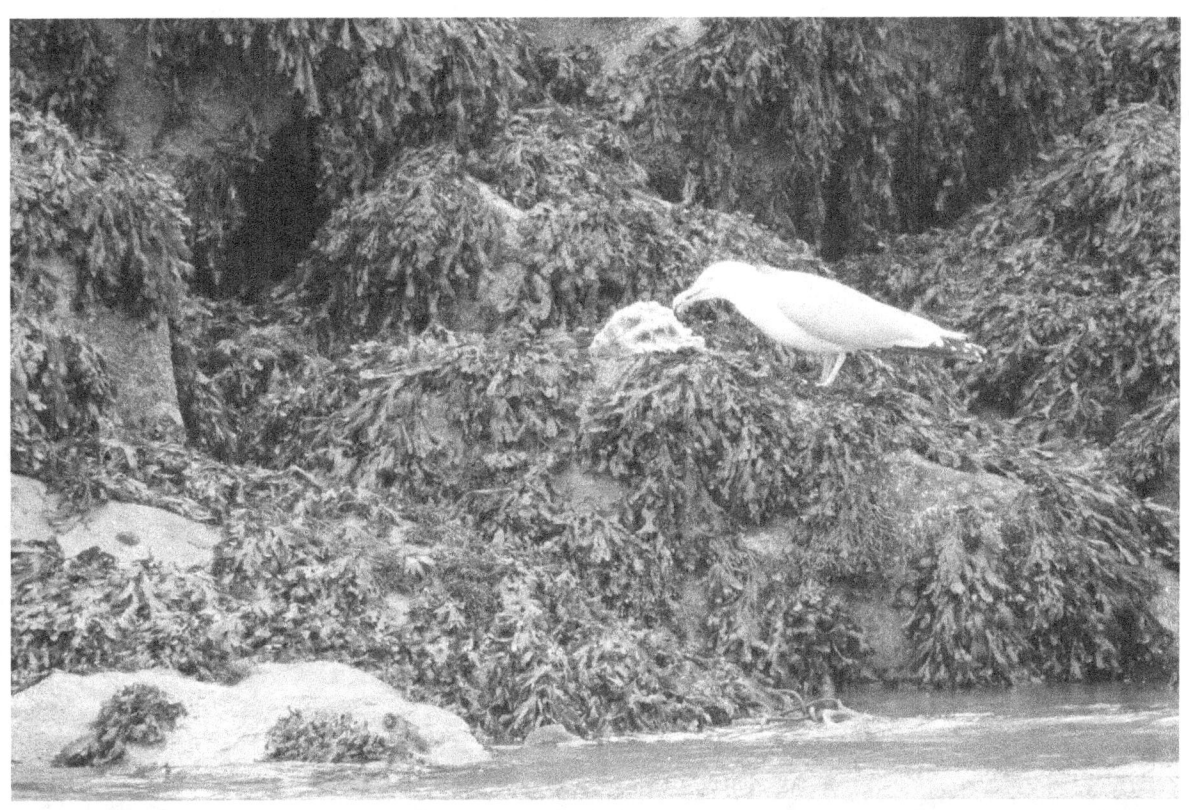

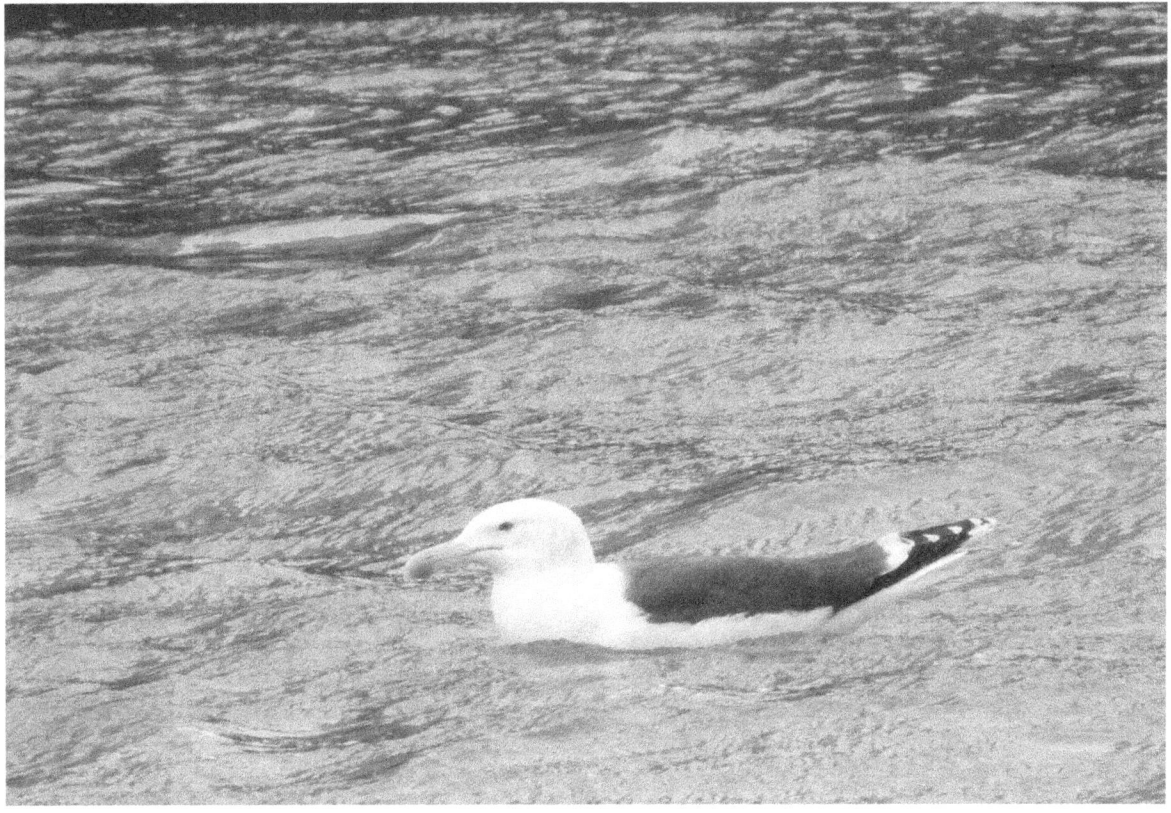

Dunmore East, Co. Waterford

Opposite (Top): From above Counsellors Strand, the Harbour can be seen (centre) in the distance.

Opposite (Bottom): Counsellors Strand pictured from High Road. A favourite beach for swimmers and sunbathers during the summer months.

Below: On the left a Great black-backed gull. Renowned for their often aggressive behaviour.

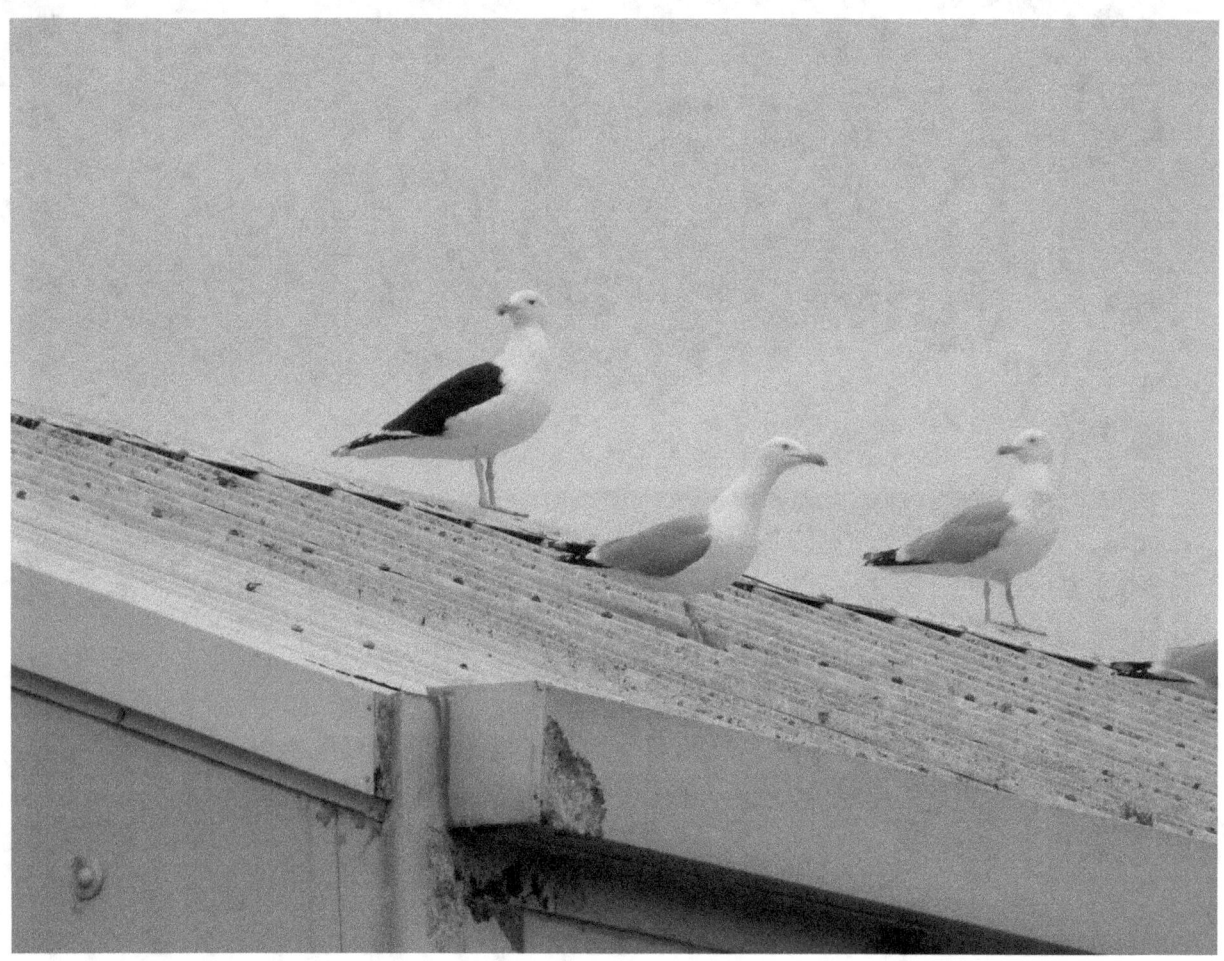

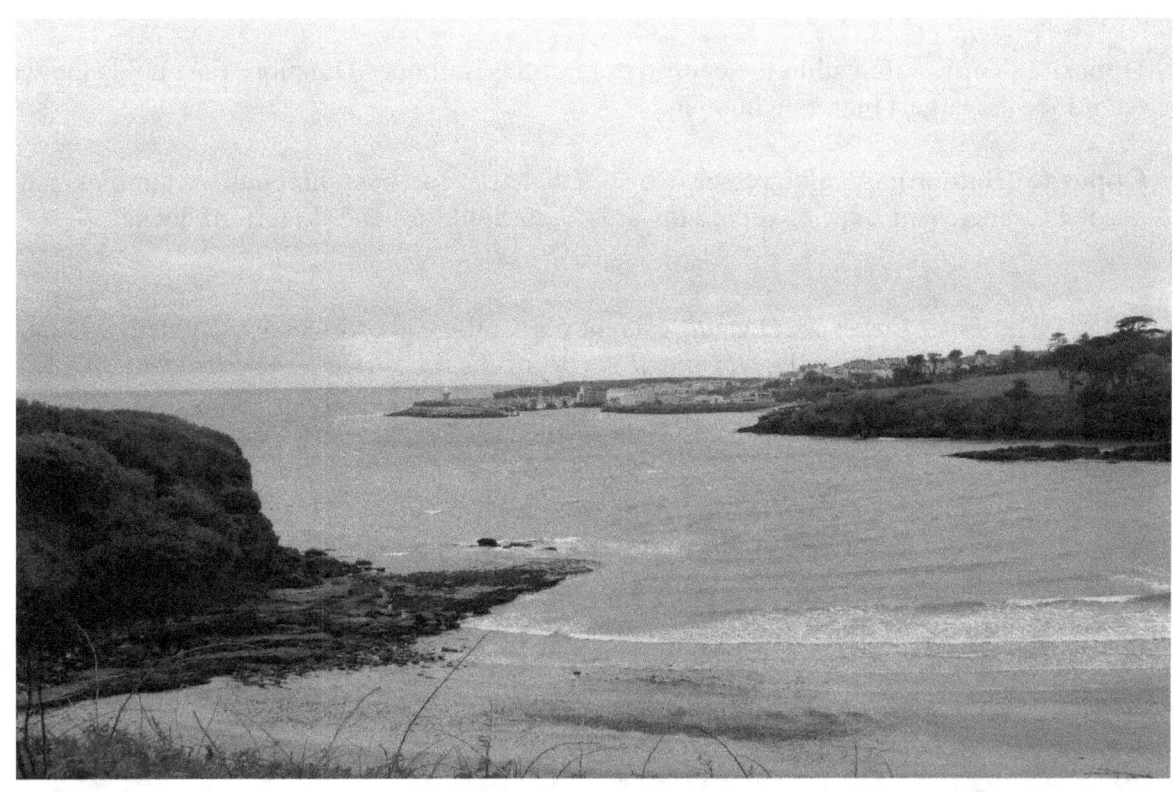

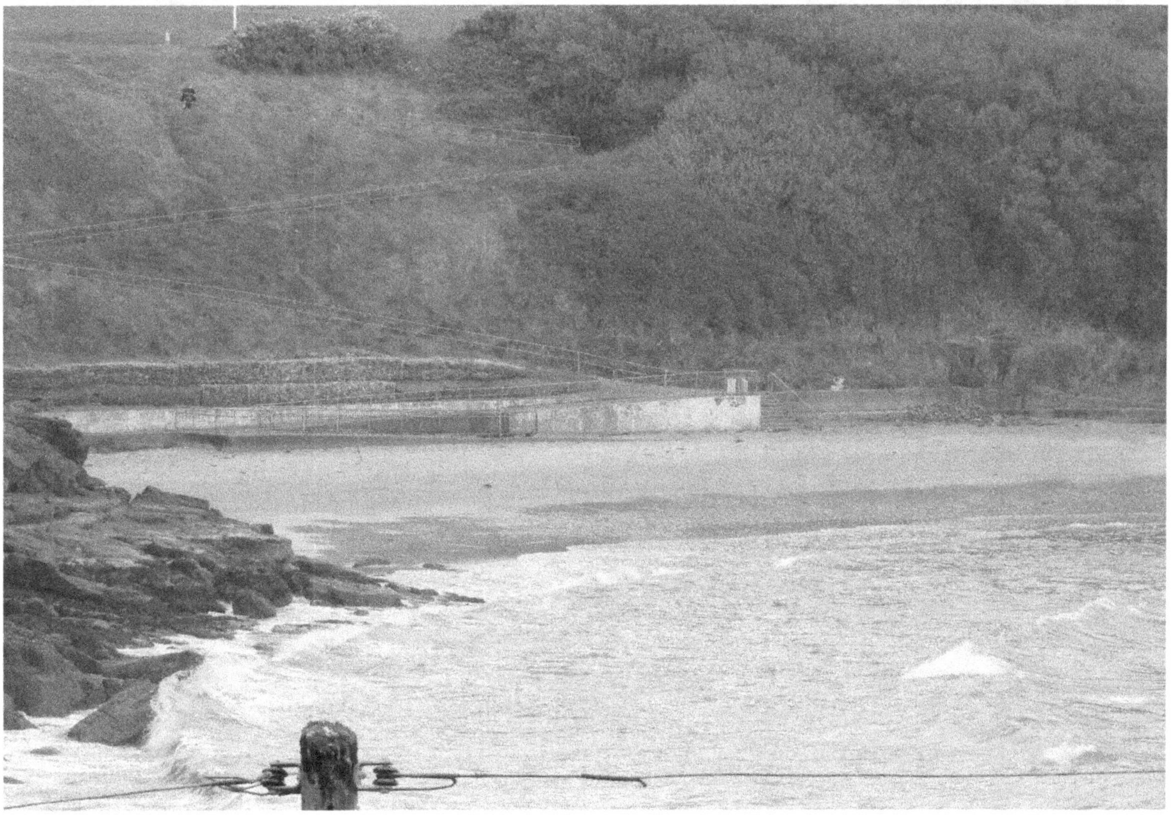

Dunmore East, Co. Waterford

Opposite (Top): Safe within the calm waters of the Harbour. Dunmore East holds the world record for the largest tuna caught on a rod.

Opposite (Bottom): A pilot vessel is also situated at the busy harbour. A familiar hand is needed for merchant ships travelling towards Waterford Port and Waterford docks.

Below: The *Dora Foster McDougal*, a Trent class all-weather lifeboat stationed at Dunmore East (2017). The *Dora Foster McDougal* is part of the relief fleet. The *Elizabeth and Ronald* is assigned to Dunmore East and came into service on the 7th October 1996.

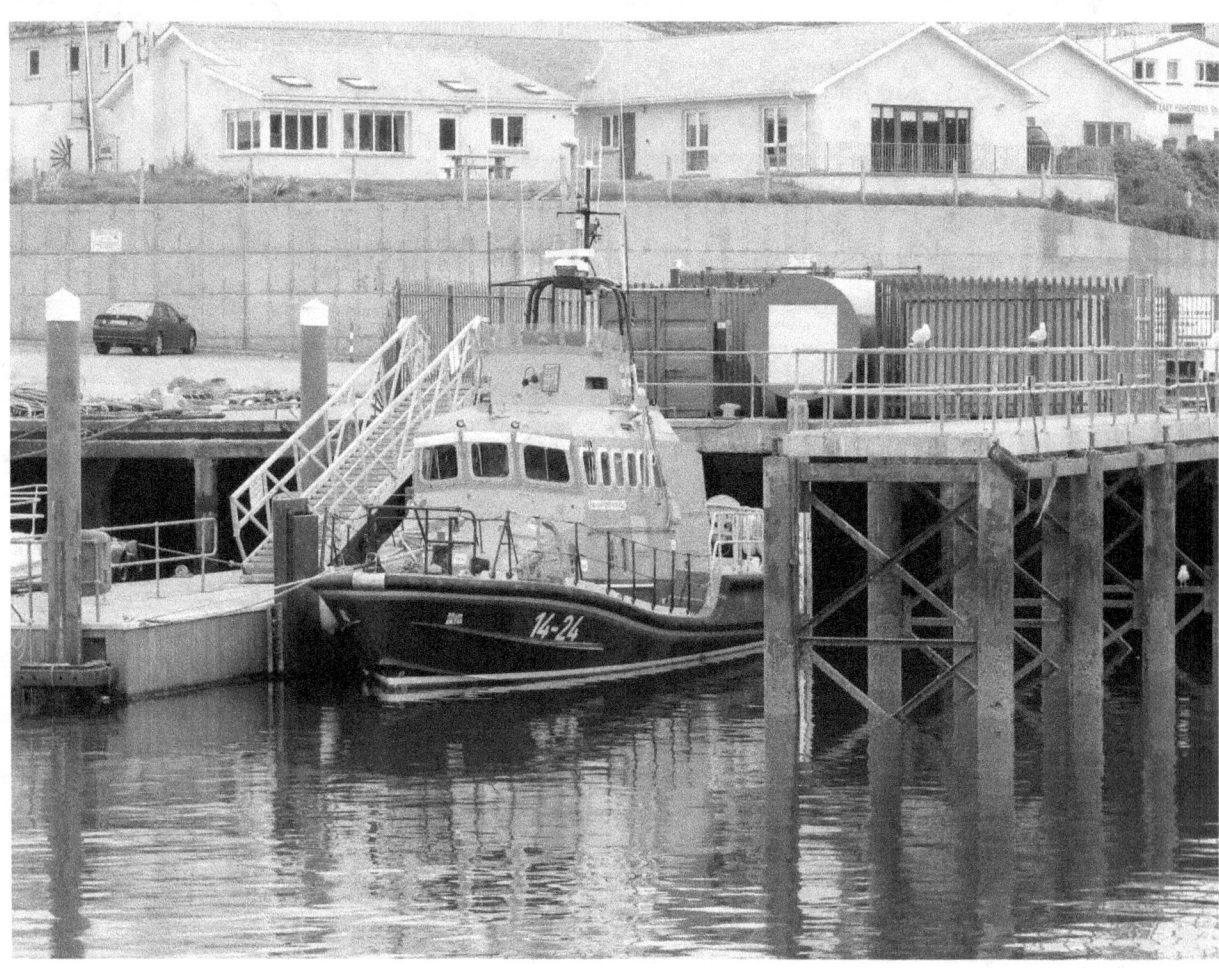

Dunmore East, Co. Waterford

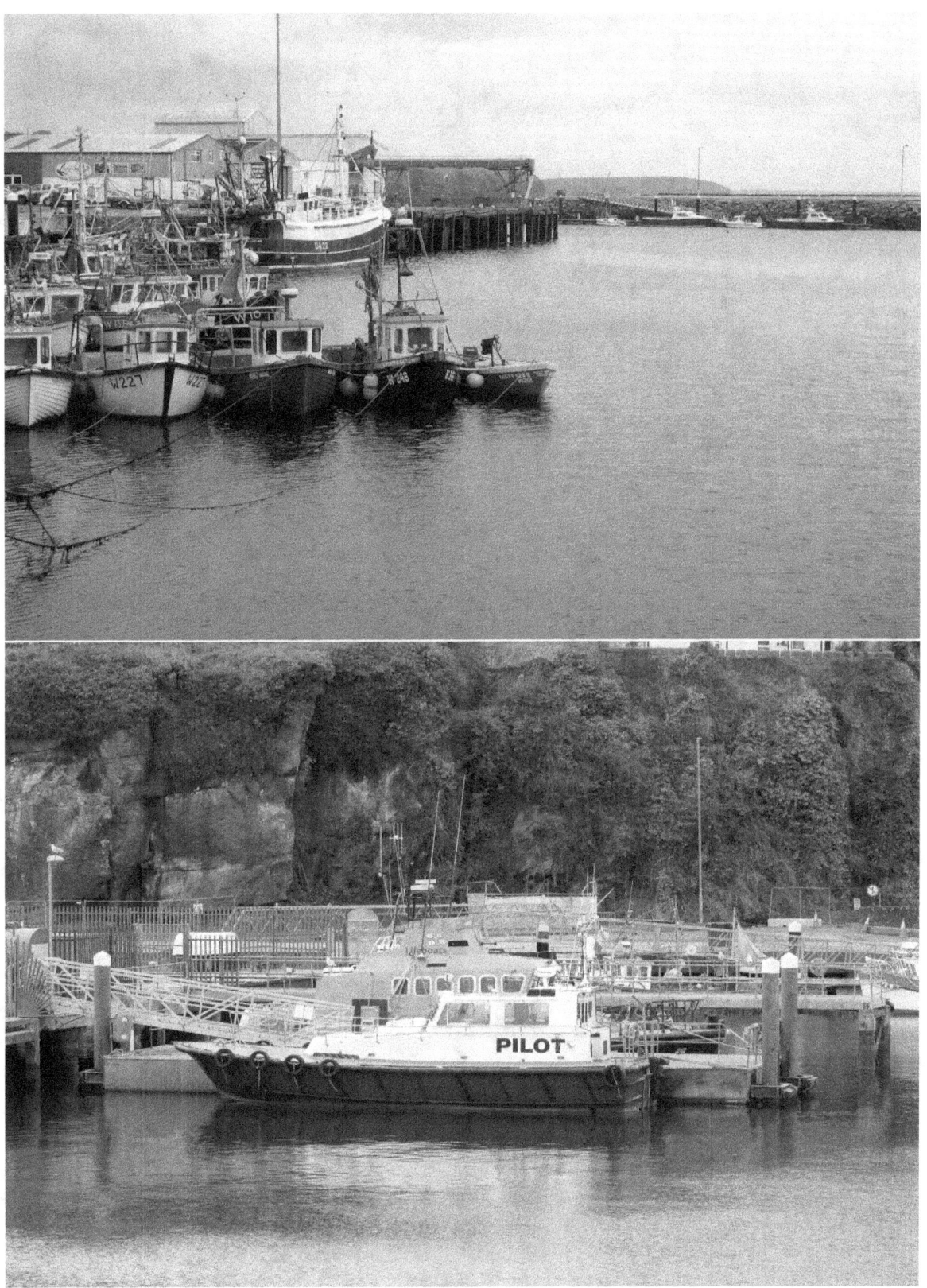

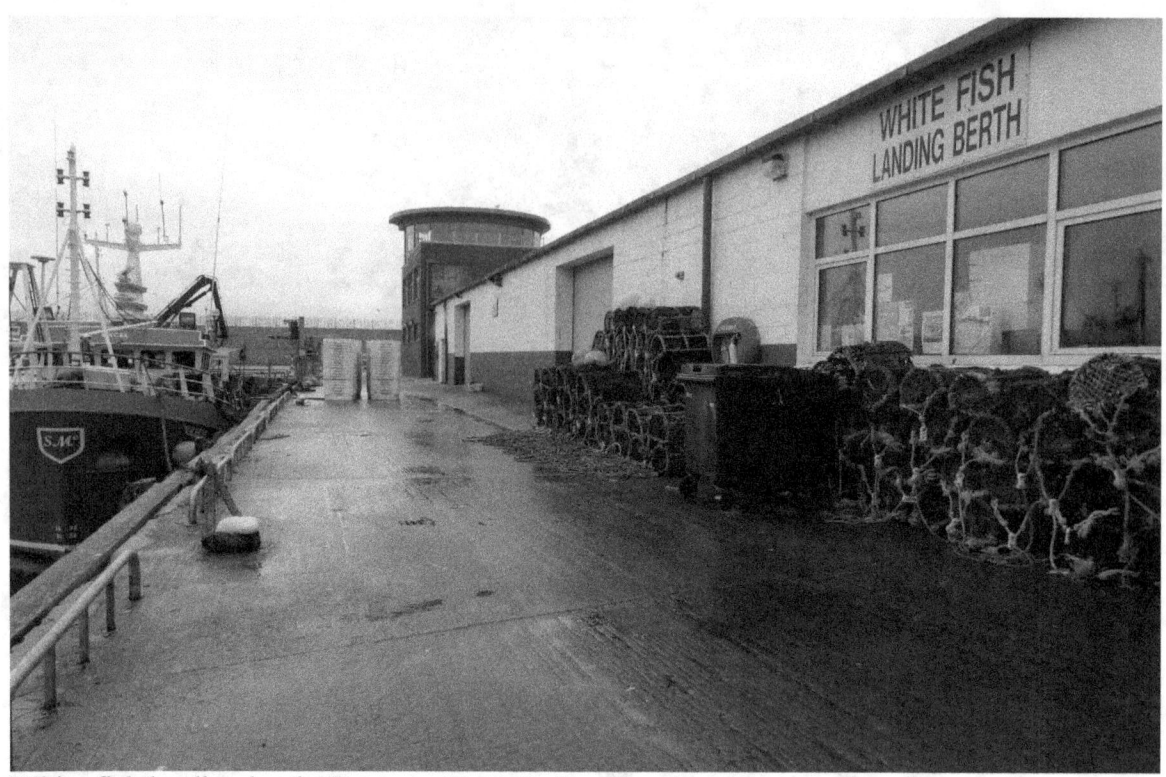

White fish loading berth, Dunmore East Harbour

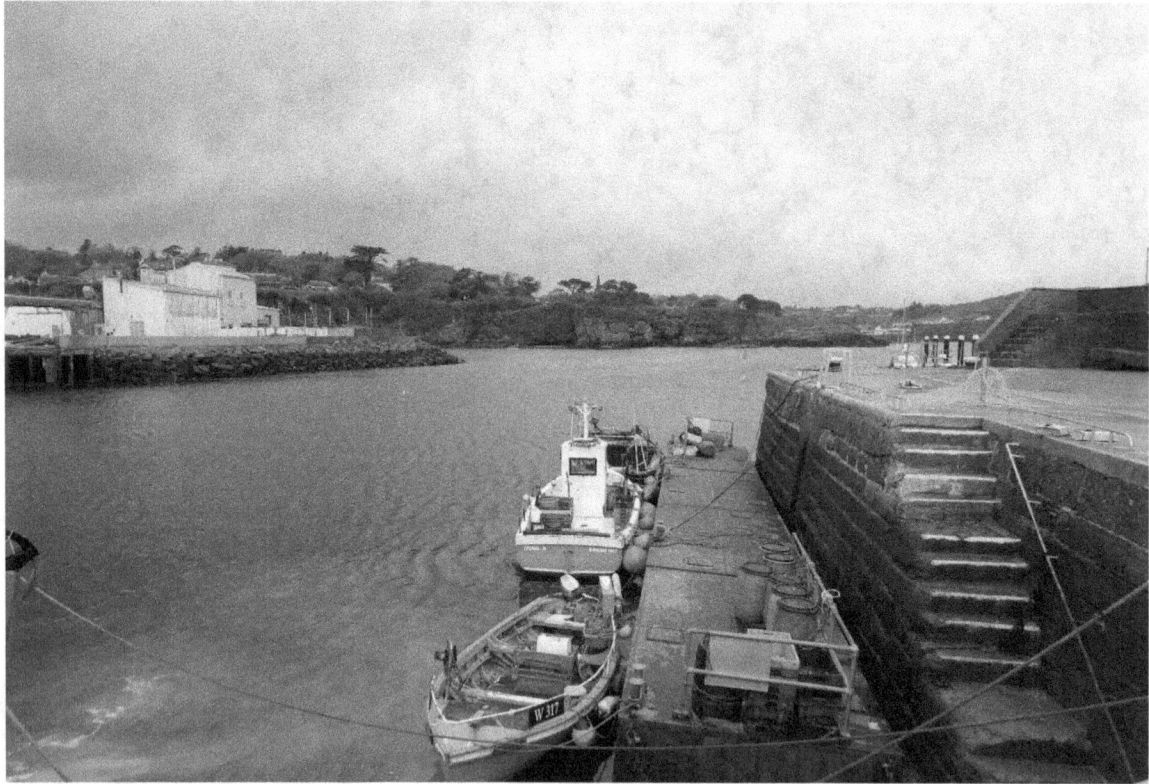

Smaller fishing boats also need their moorings.

Dunmore East, Co. Waterford

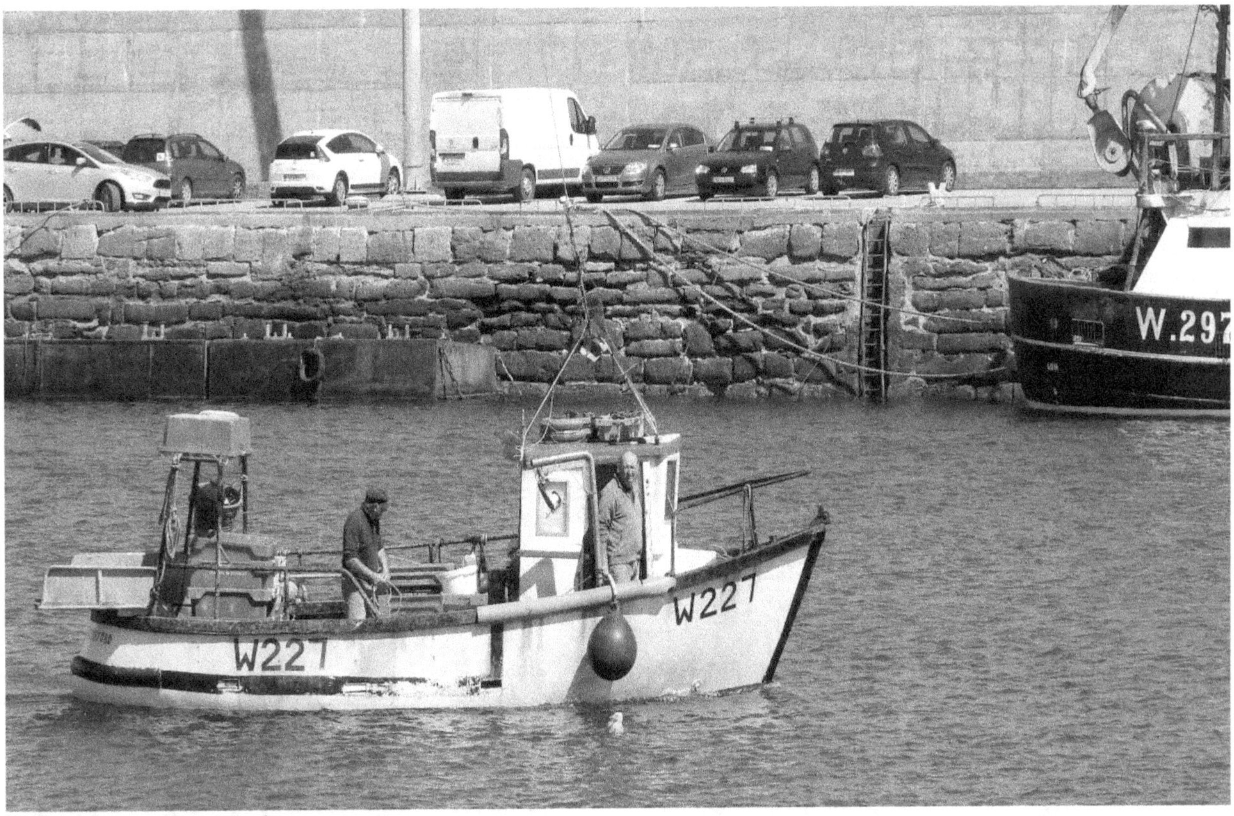

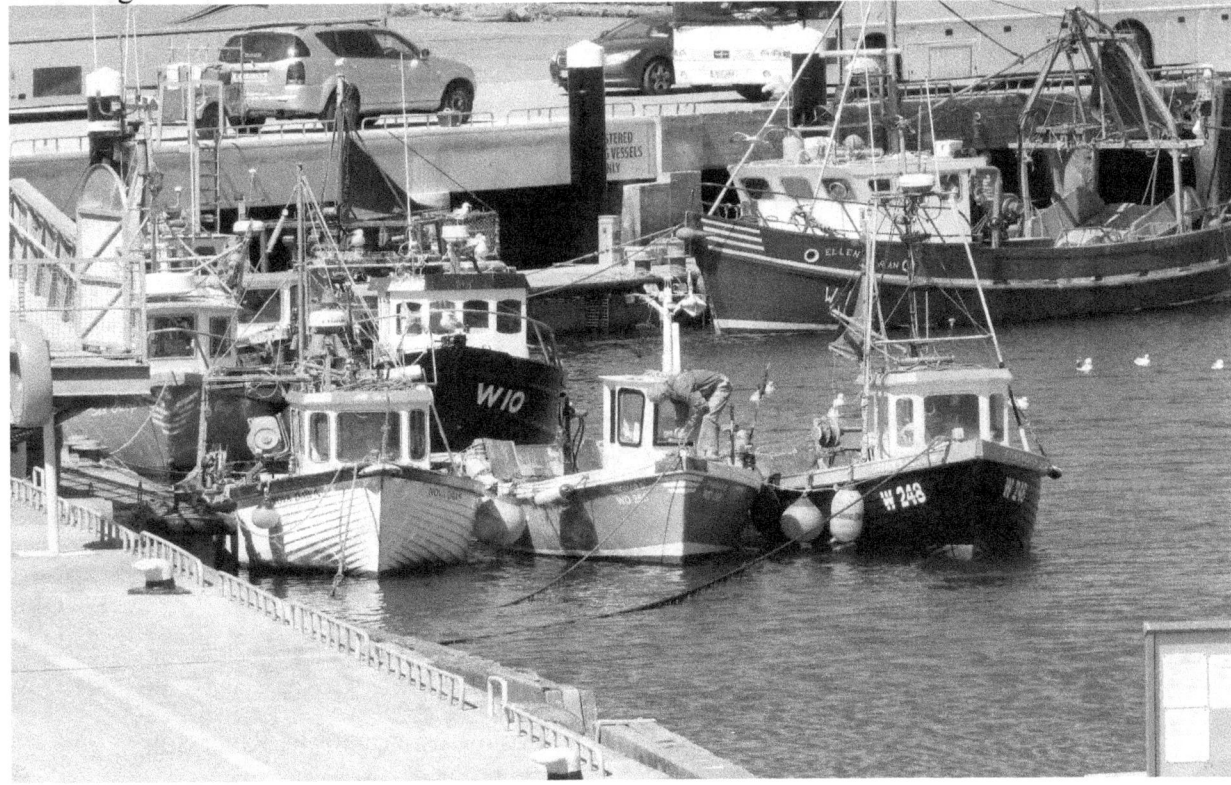

Returning to the Harbour

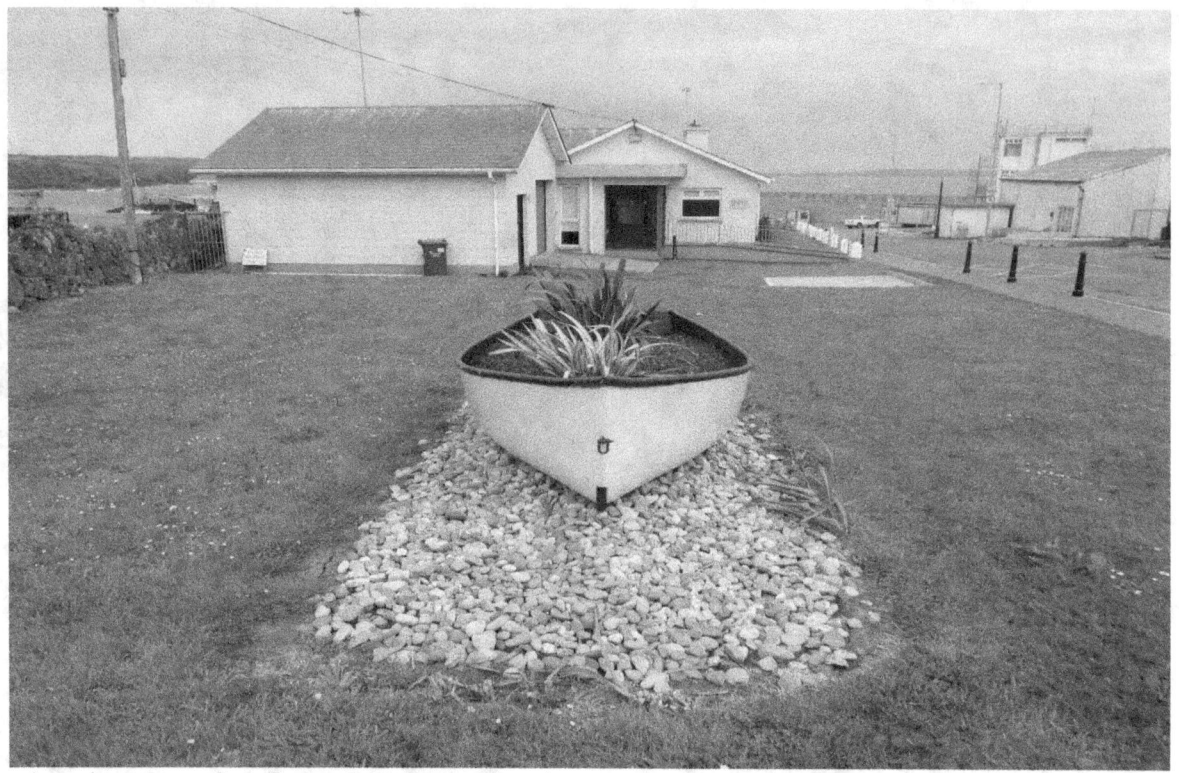

A maintenance free flower bed pictured at the entrance to the harbour.

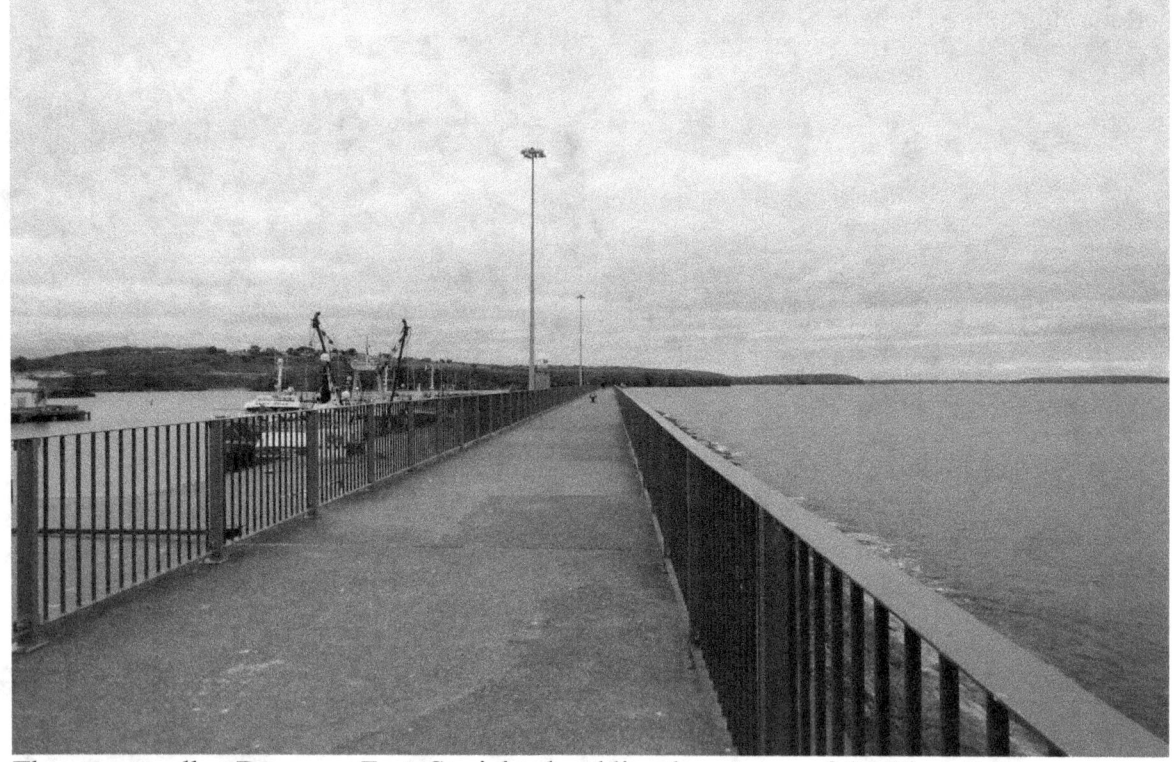

The storm wall at Dunmore East. Straight ahead lies the estuary of the River Suir.

Dunmore East, Co. Waterford

Below: Returning to the Harbour in the afternoon.

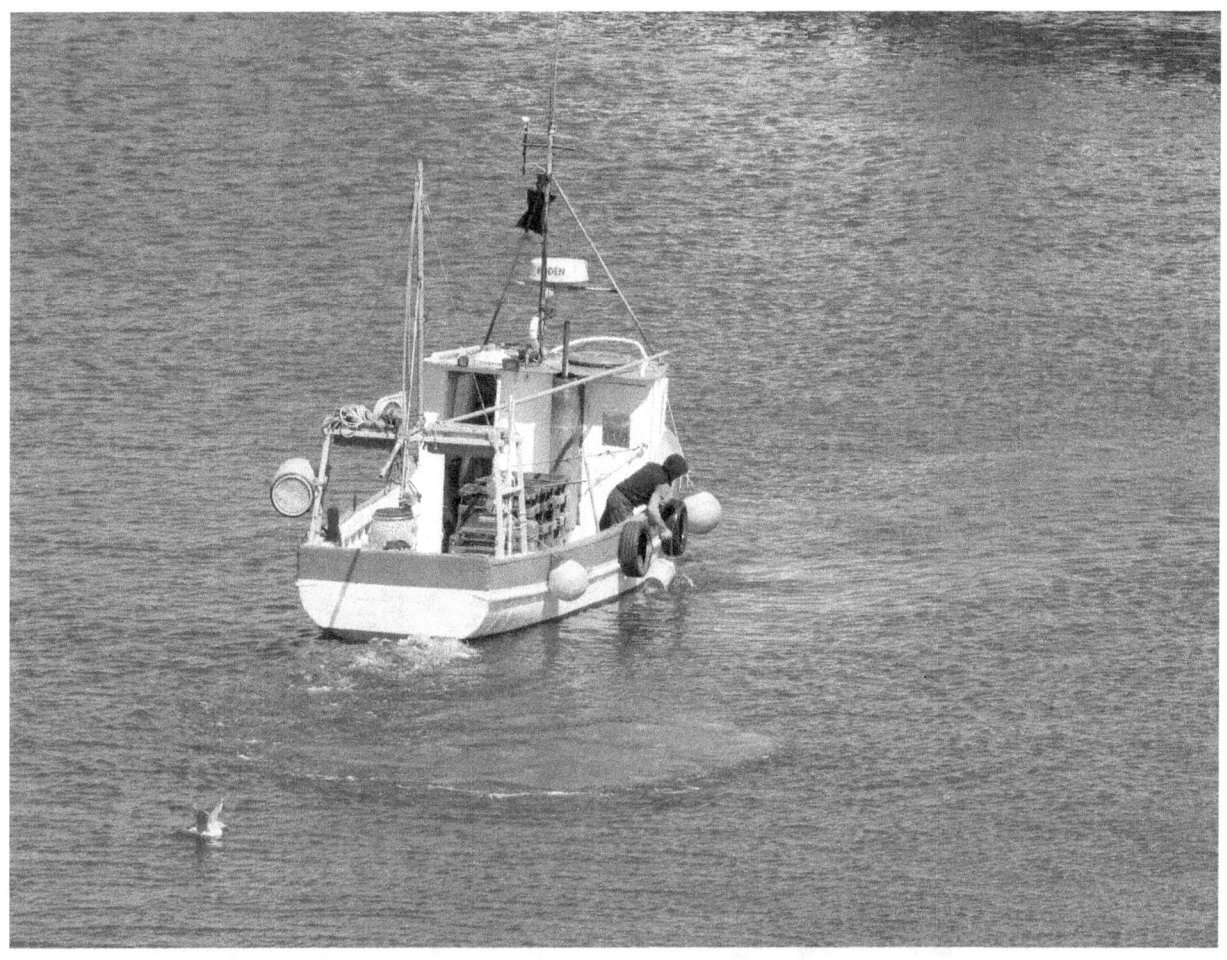

Dunmore East, Co. Waterford

Opposite (Top): The village pump, a reminder of days gone by. Displayed are the blue and white colours of County Waterford.

Opposite (Bottom): The old school located in Killea. Who left the gate open?

Dunmore East, Co. Waterford

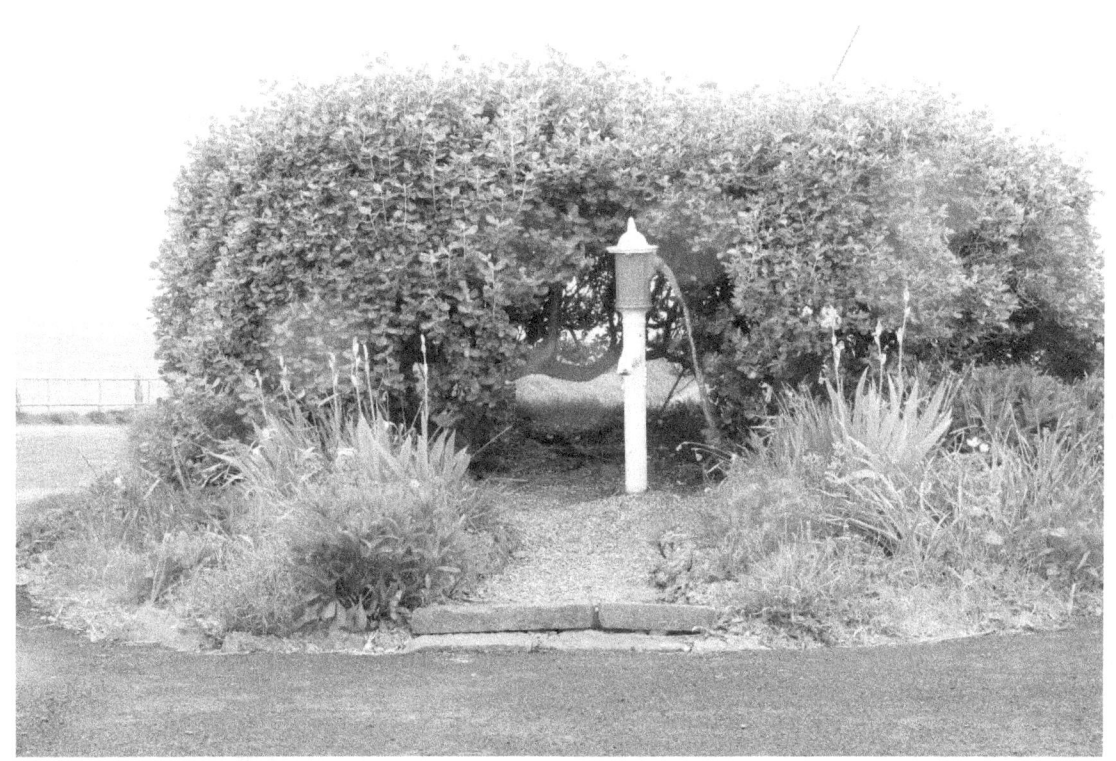

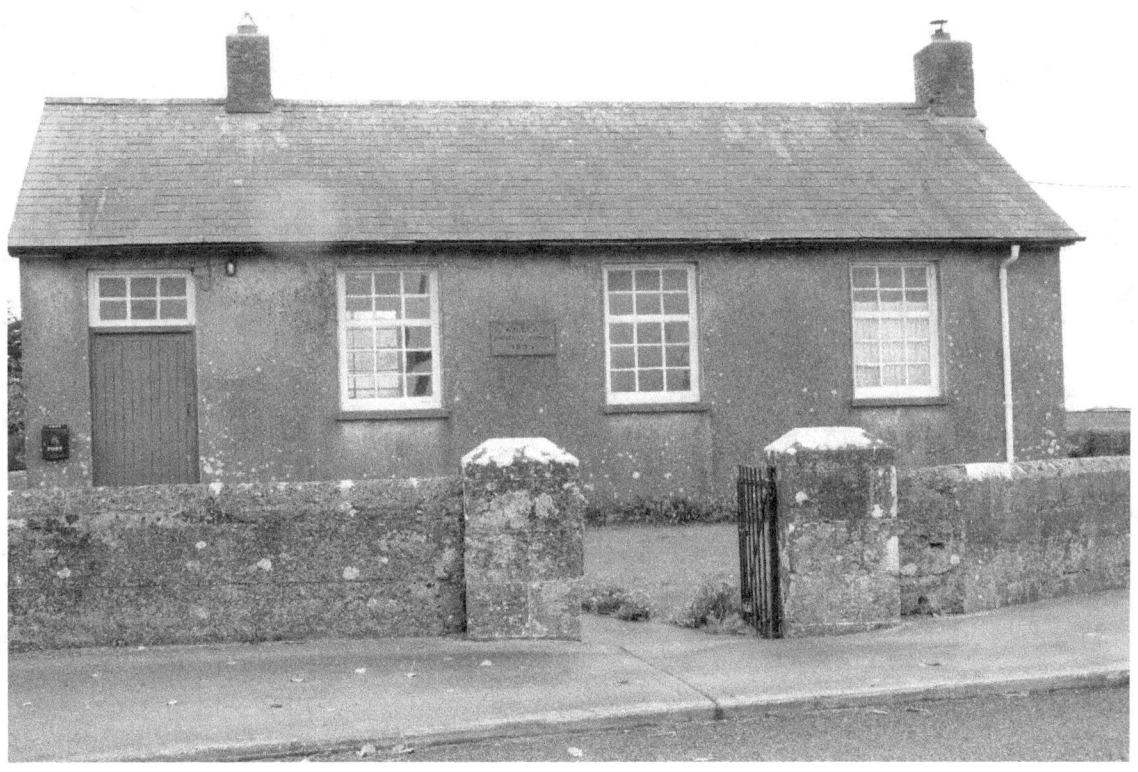

Opposite (Top): The many steps up to the Haven Hotel. With pristine front lawns, it makes an ideal location on a summer's day.

Opposite (Bottom): St. Andrew's Church situated opposite the People's Park. The church spire stands at 115 feet high.

Below: Formerly known as *The Ship*, the *Azzurro* bar and restaurant is situated at the corner of High Road.

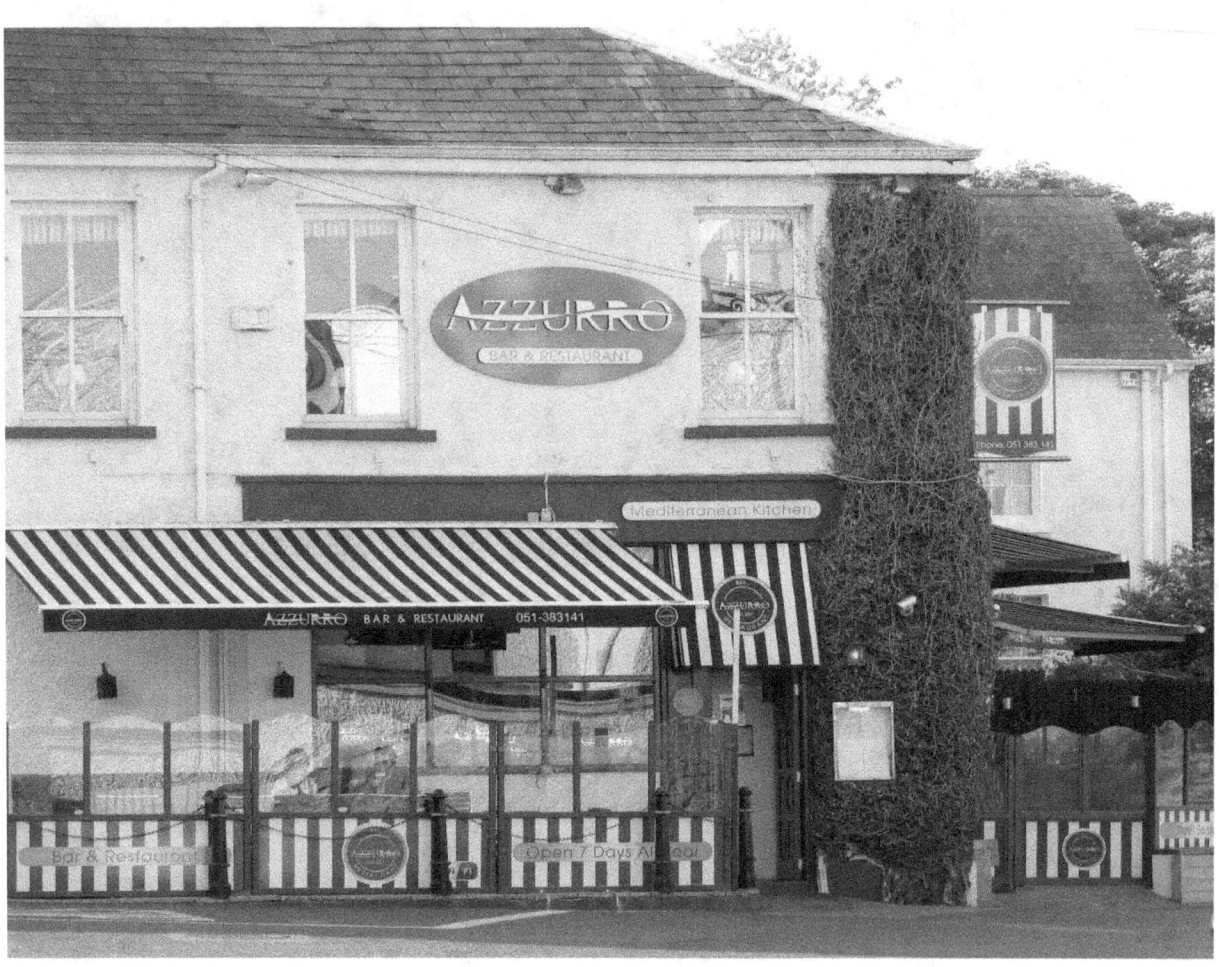

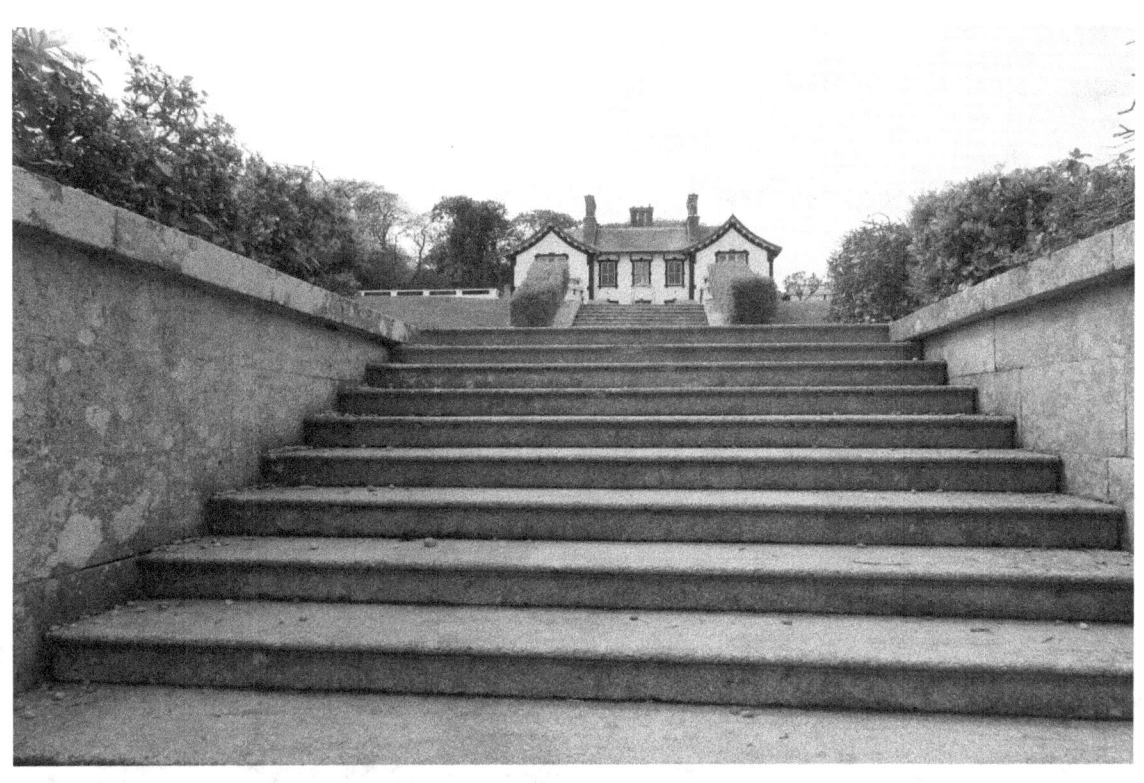

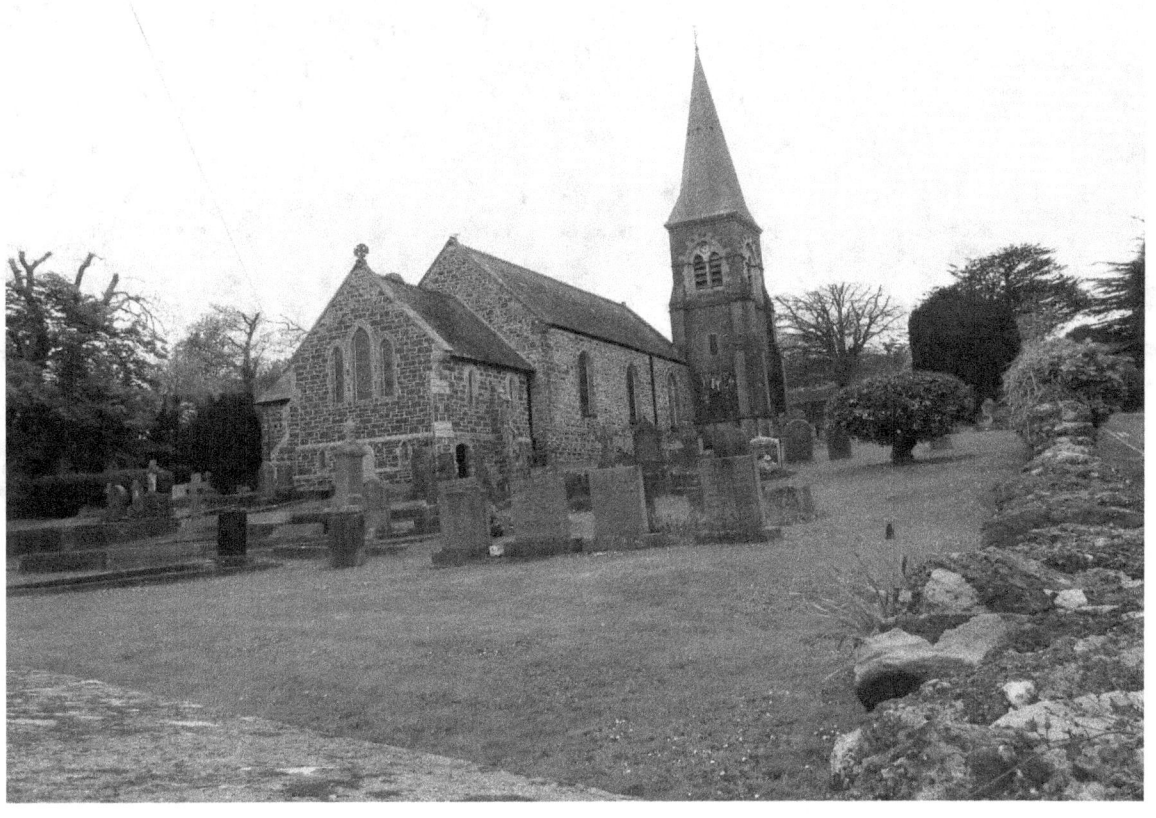

Dunmore East, Co. Waterford

Opposite (Top): The fire station, currently home to two fire tenders.

Opposite (Bottom): *Hayes Pub* situated in Killea (next to the Roman Catholic church). No Dogs allowed!

Below: Inside the *Spinnaker Bar*, located in the Lower Village of Dunmore East.

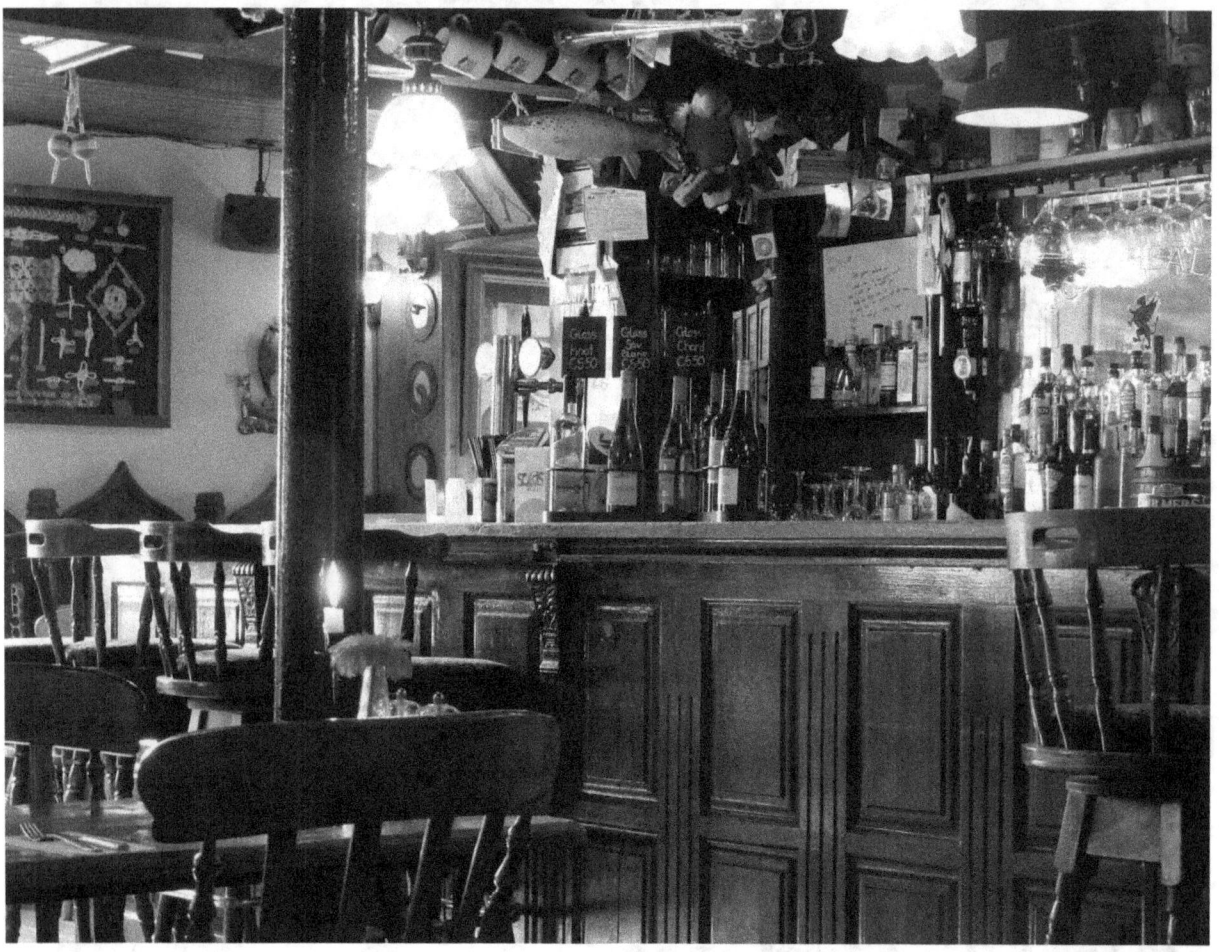

Dunmore East, Co. Waterford

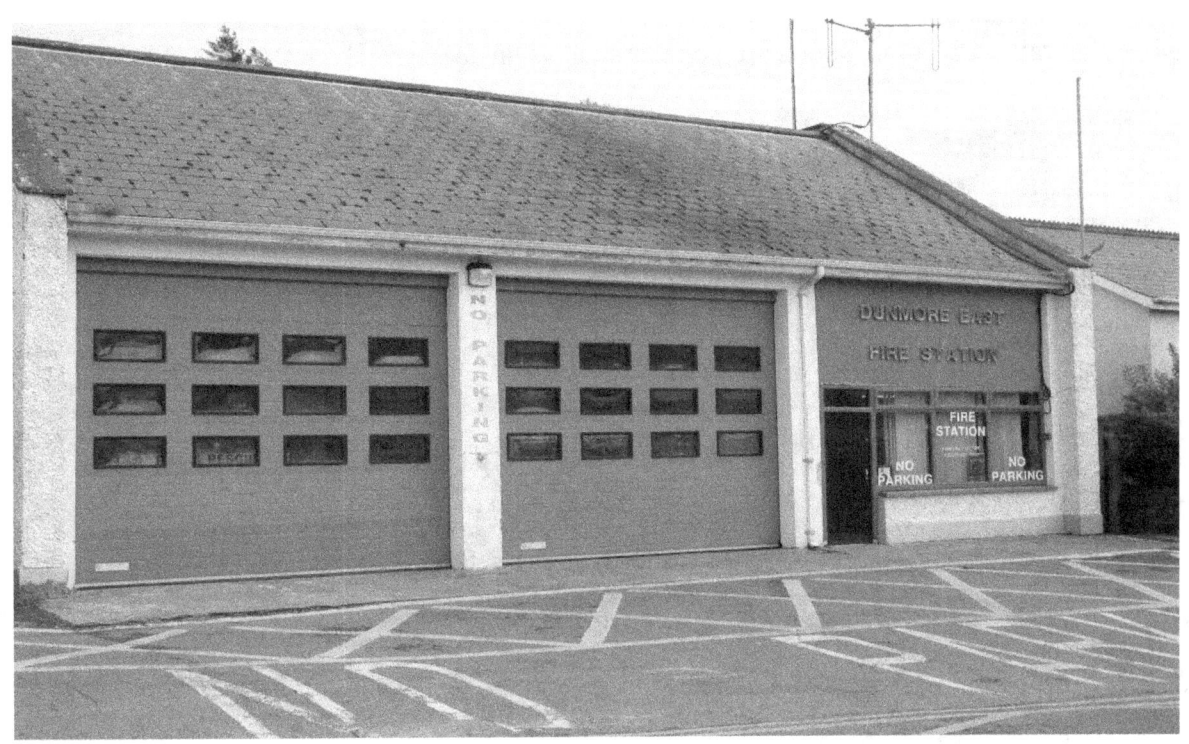

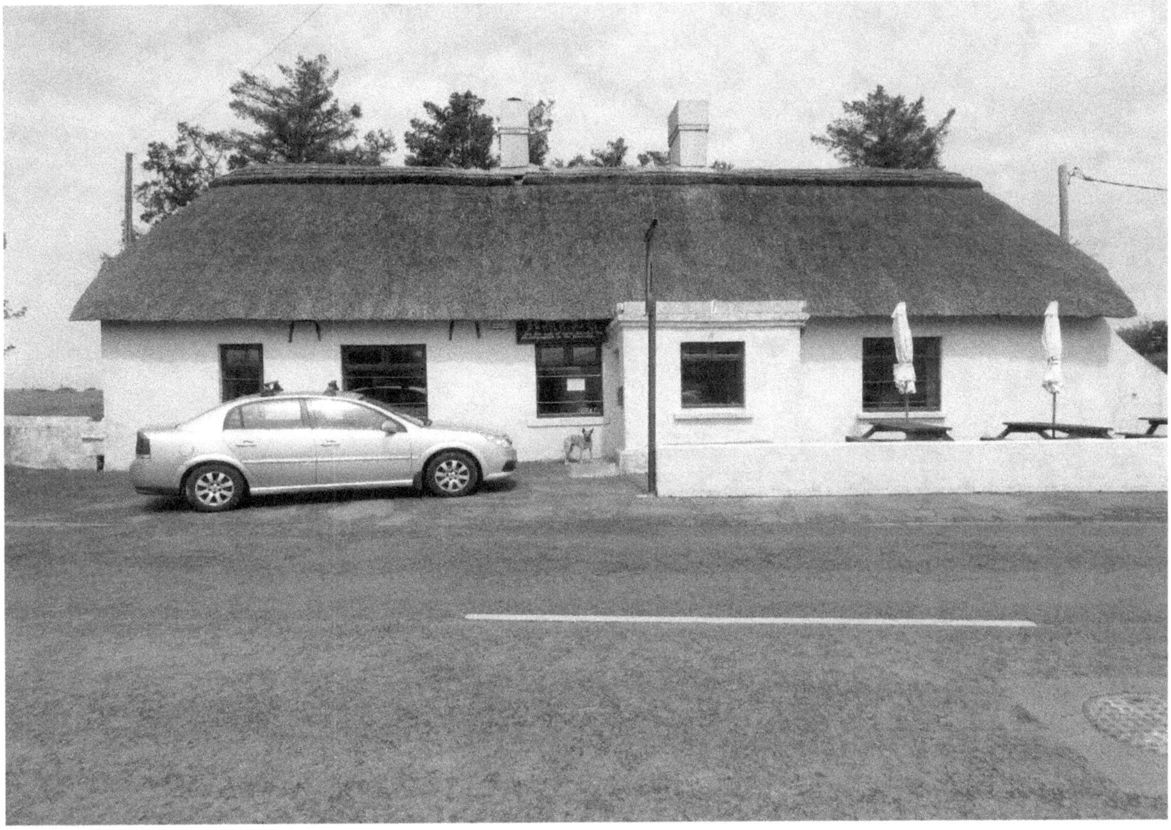

Dunmore East, Co. Waterford

Below: Naturally, adventure sports are popular such as kayaking.

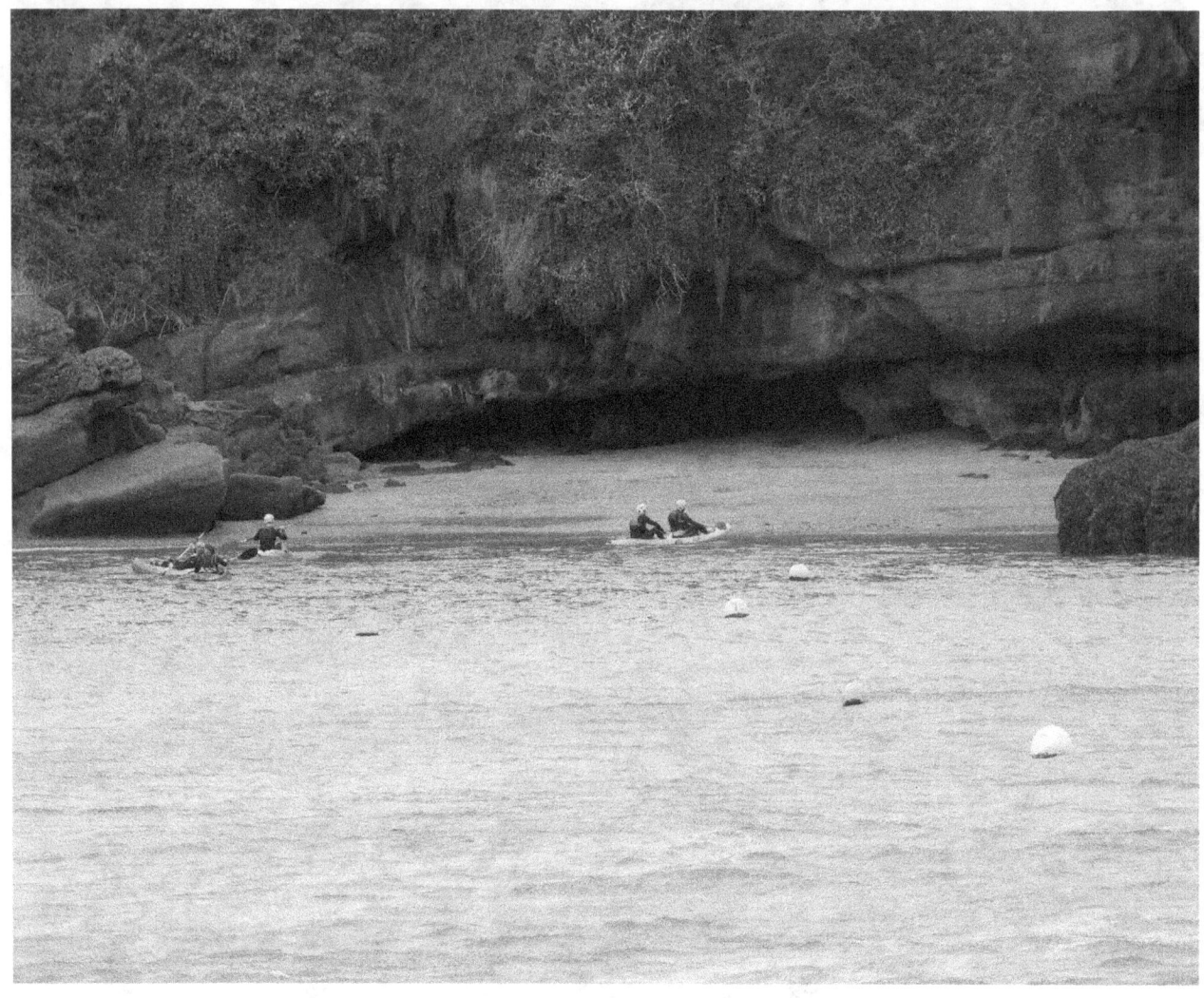

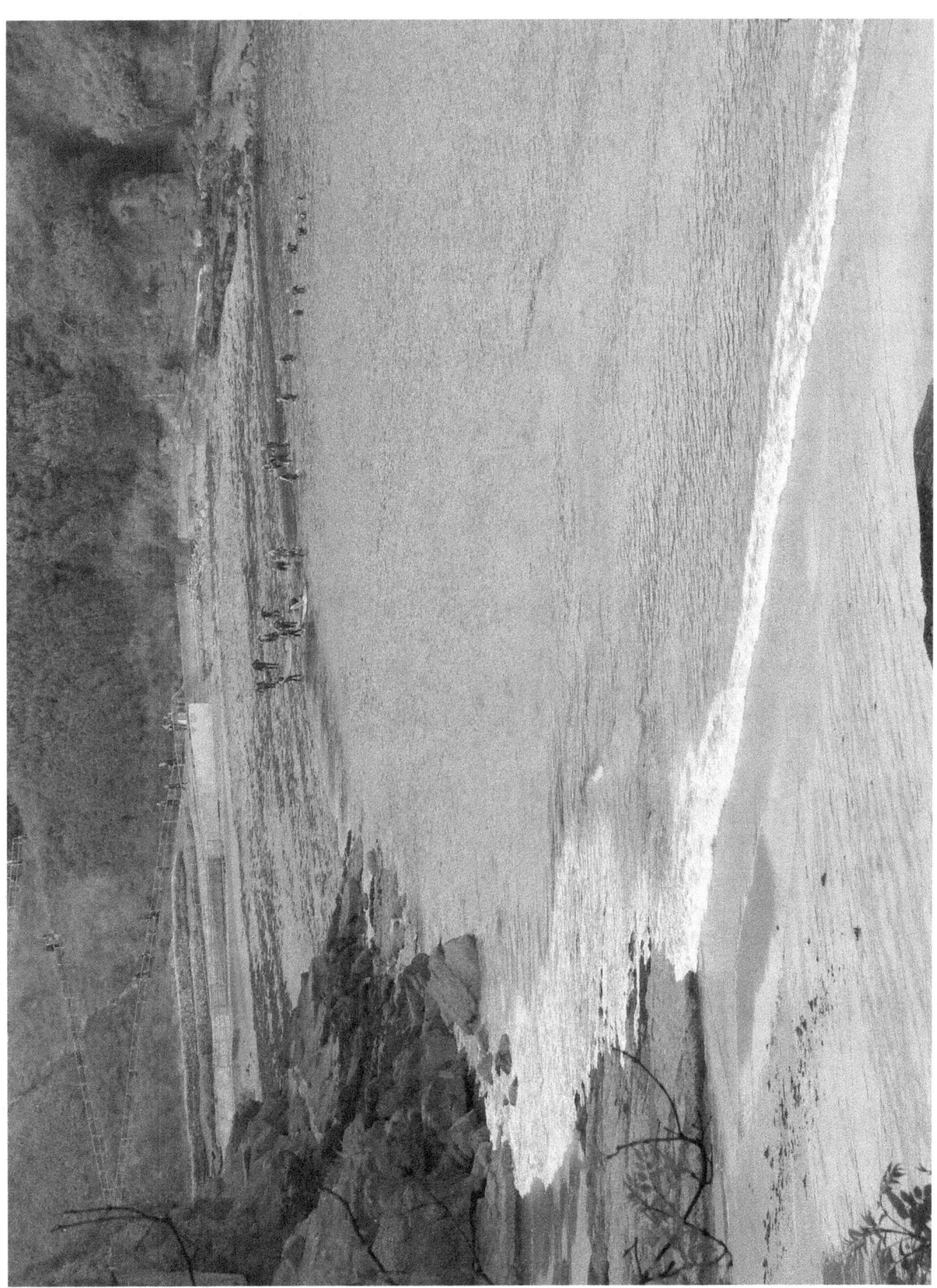

Dunmore East, Co. Waterford

Opposite (Top): The village is home to a post office. The service is complemented by at least three post boxes in different locations throughout the village.

Opposite (Bottom): The ruined church of Killea (Cill Aodha), built in the twelfth century. The ruins are located opposite *Holy Cross Catholic Church*.

Below: *Holy Cross Catholic Church* (Killea), built in 1817, has a traditional cruciform plan. The interior of the church has remained substantially unaltered since the Second Vatican Council (1963 - 1965). Features include the timber gallery and first floor on cast-iron pillars.

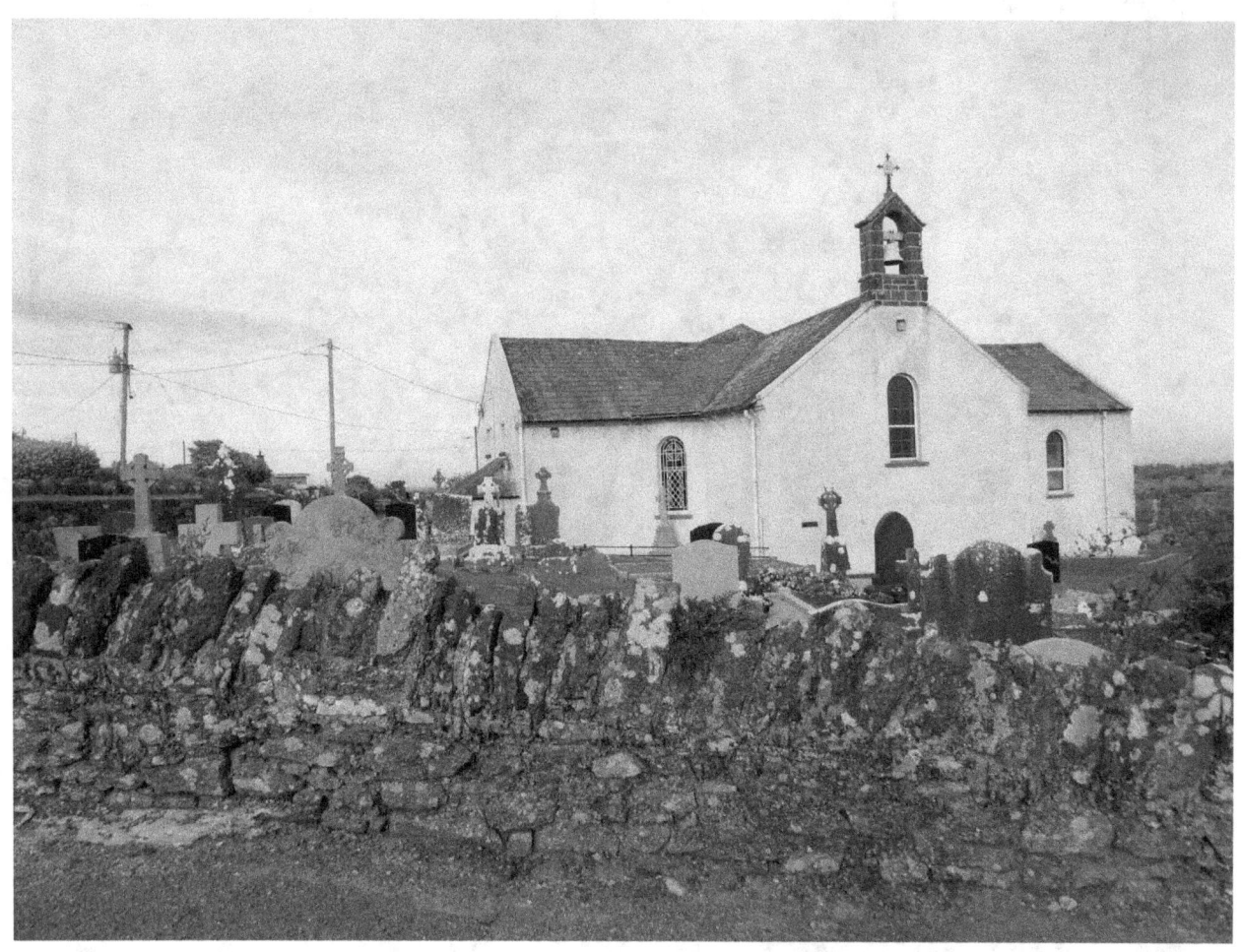

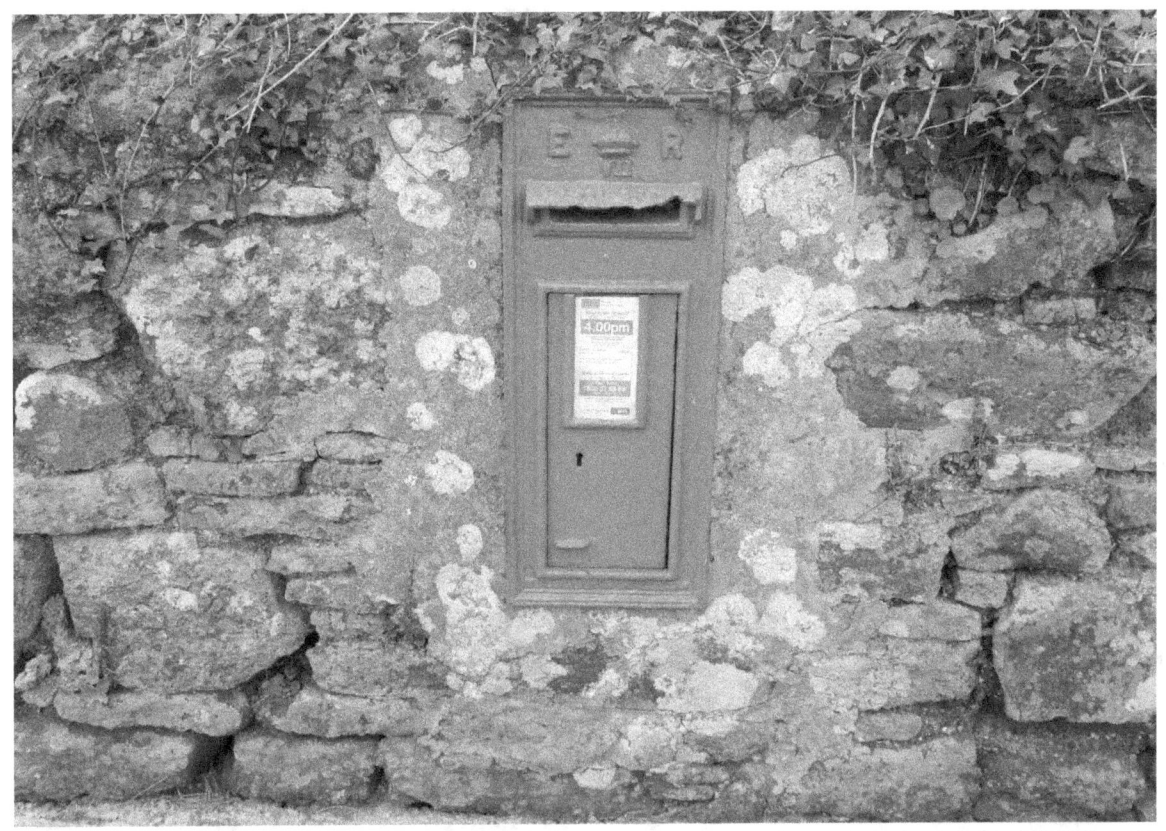

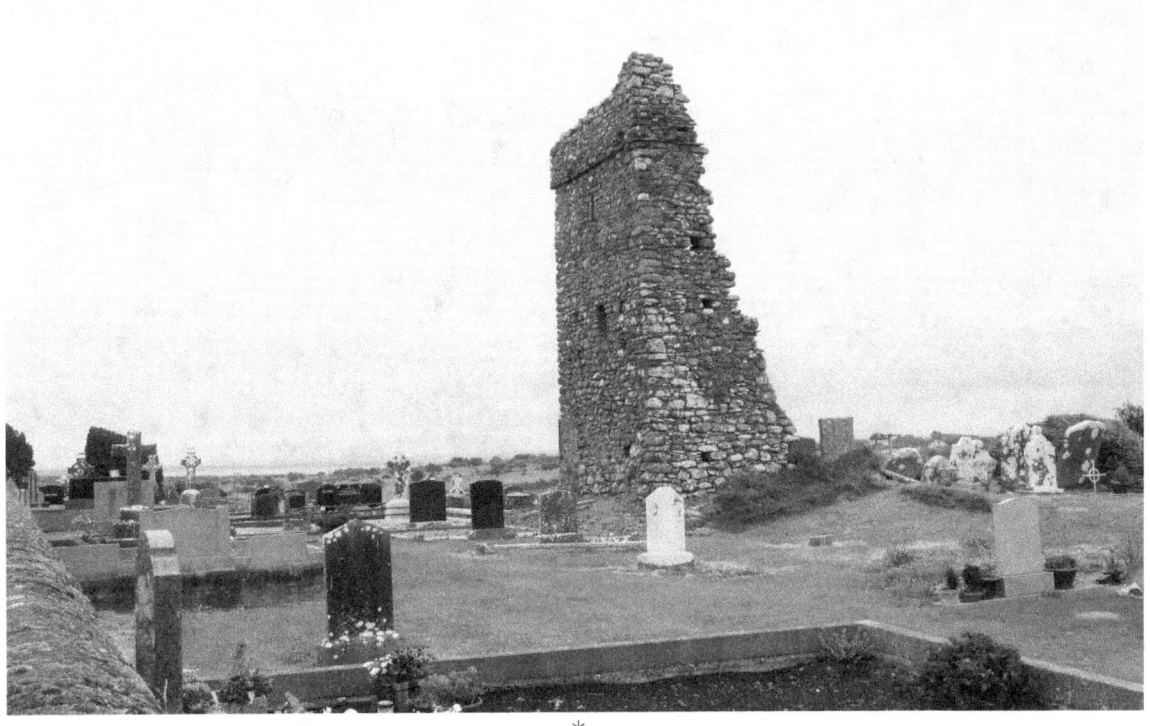

*

Dunmore East, Co. Waterford

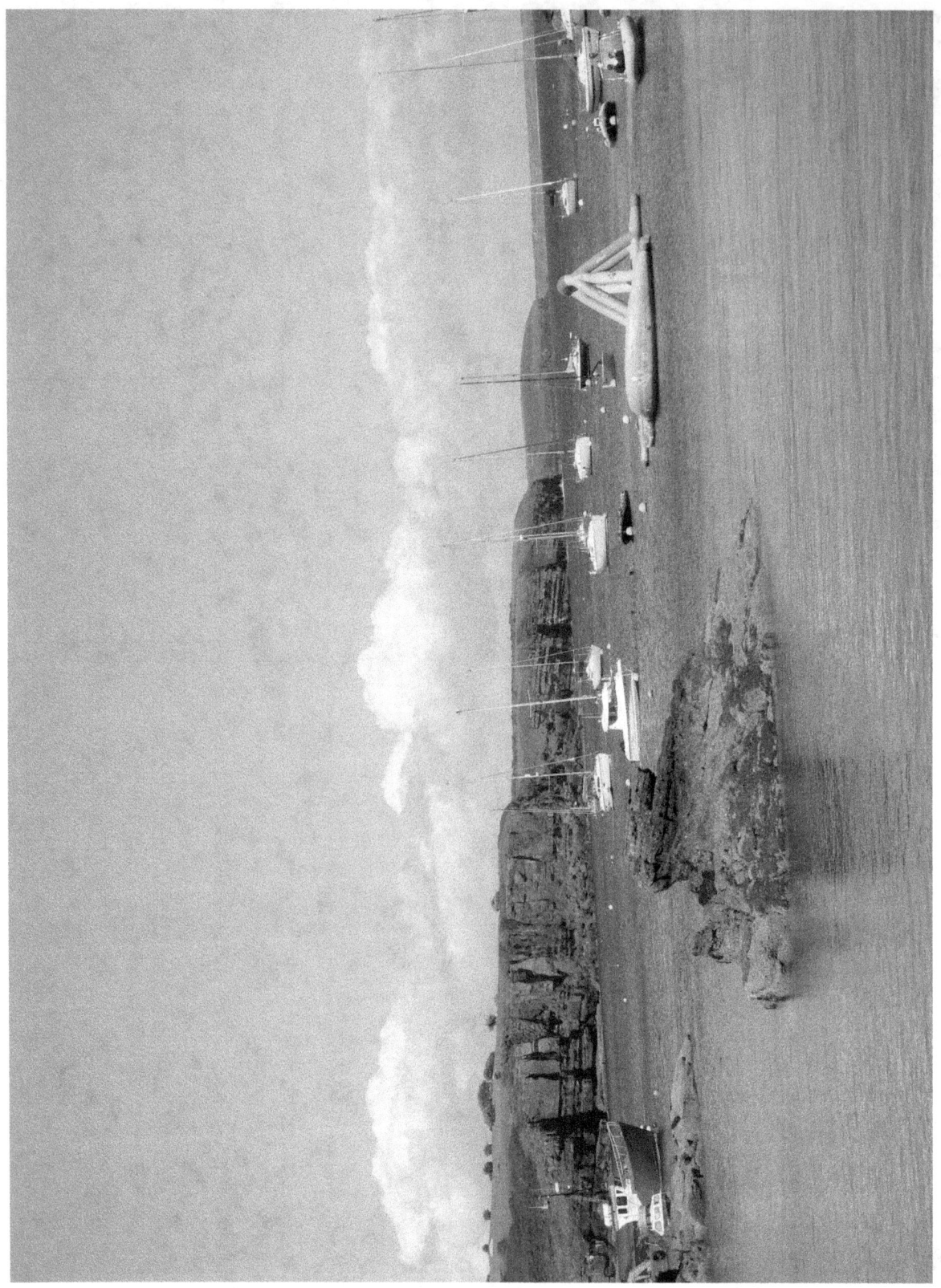

Opposite: Around the end of May the number of sailboats anchored increases with the anticipation of good weather for June until September.

Dunmore East Woods

In 1924, John Charles de le Poer granted Dunmore East Woods and Park in a trust for the recreational use of the people of Dunmore East. The walk is approximately 3km and can be completed in 45 minutes.

The walk can be started at the High Road entrance (shown opposite) or from the Coxtown entrance. Starting at the High Road entrance which is located close to St. Andrew's church, the trail winds its way uphill coming to Cuckaloo Hill. From this point onwards the incline decreases making the trek towards Coxtown a little easier.

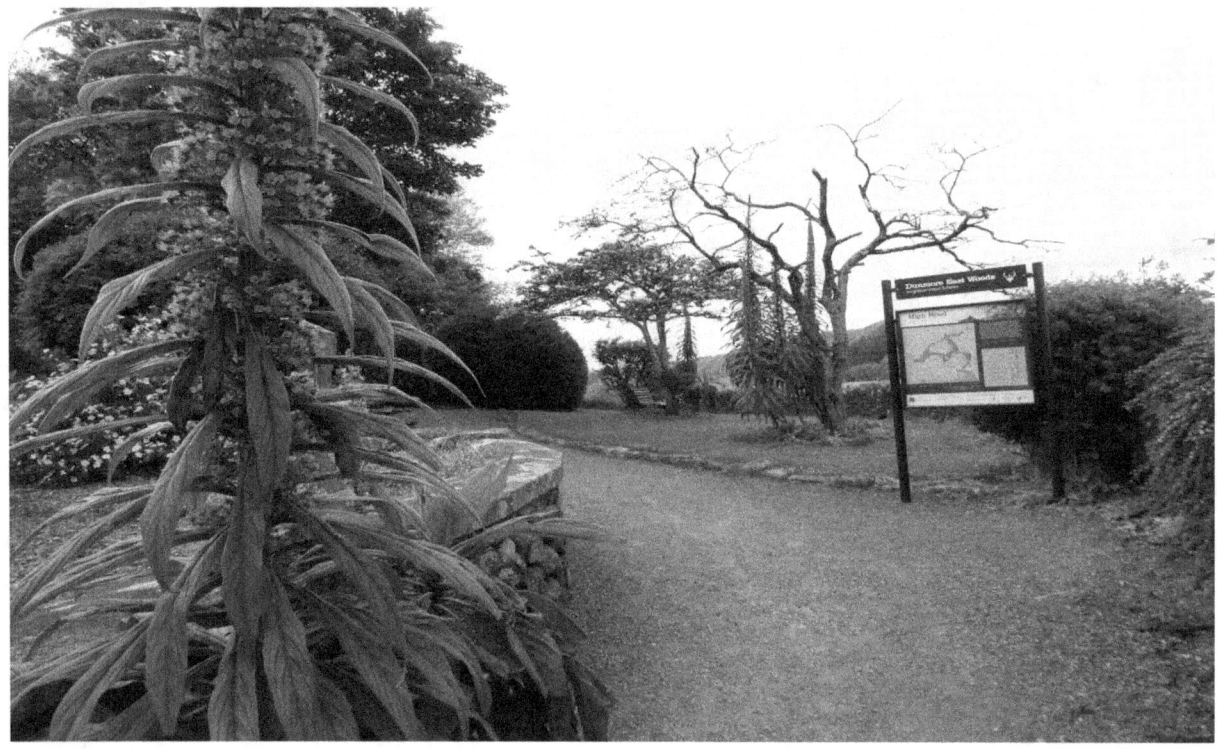

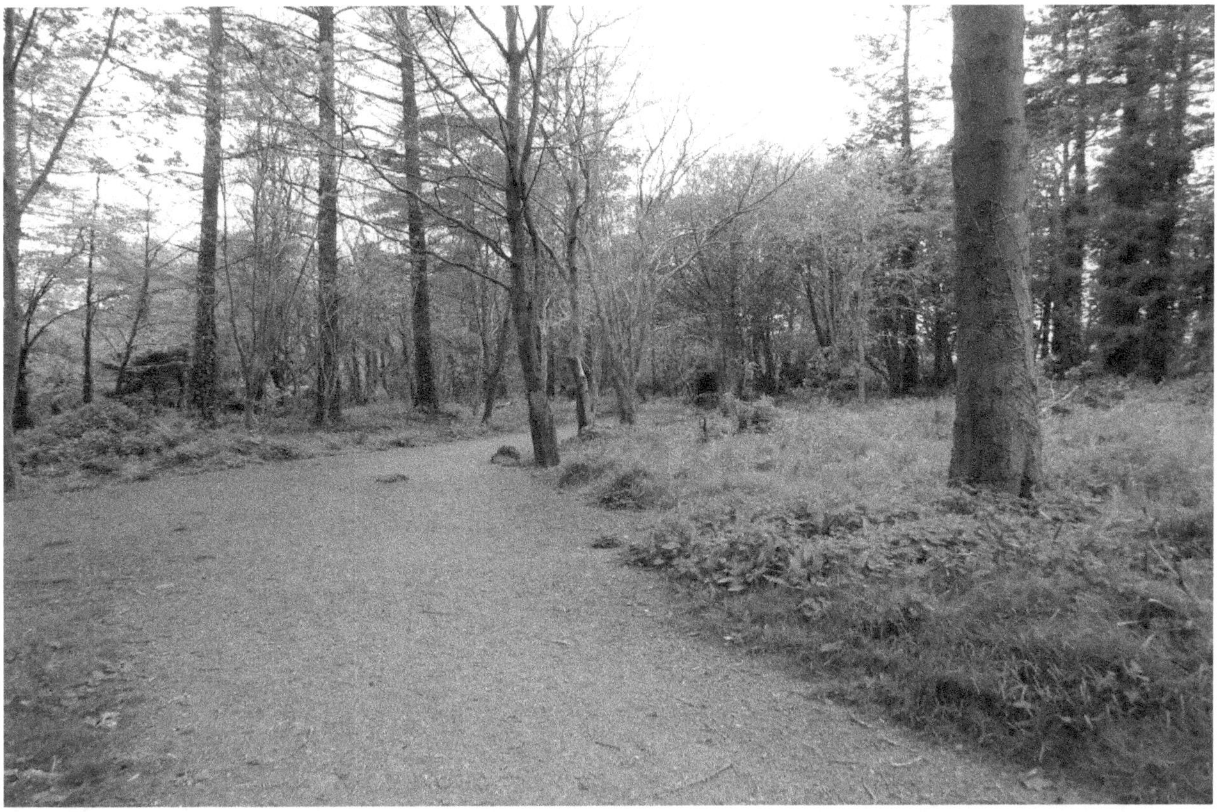

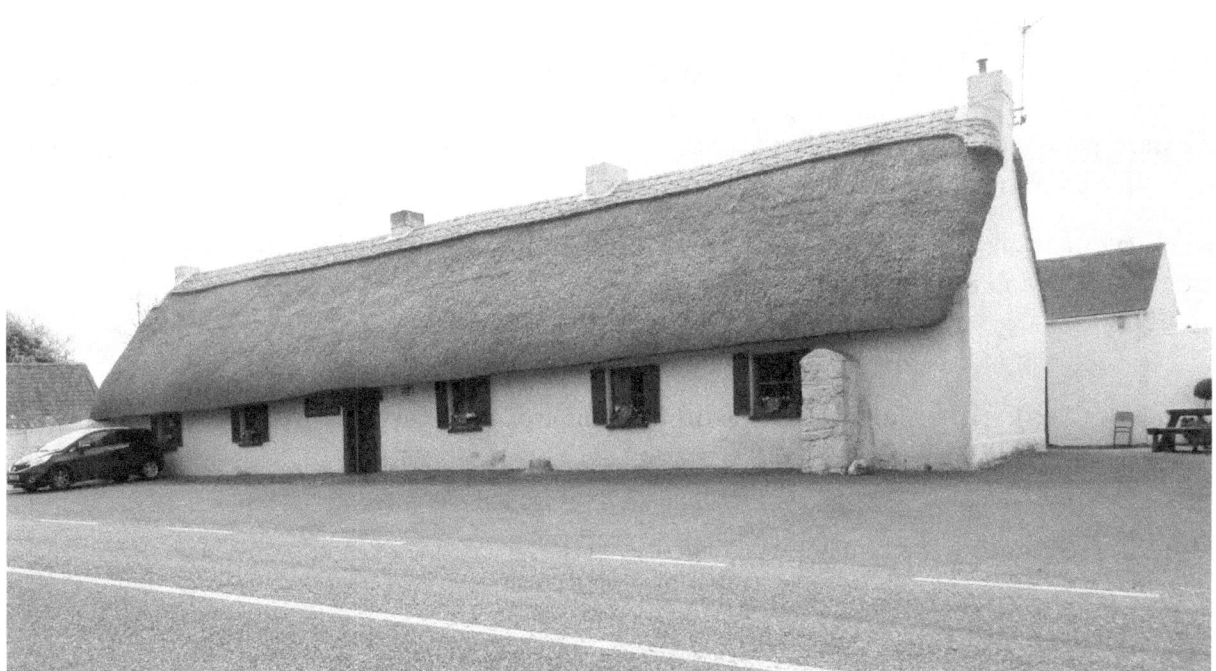

Kennedy's Bar, located on the main Waterford to Dunmore East Road.

Dunmore East Cliff Walk

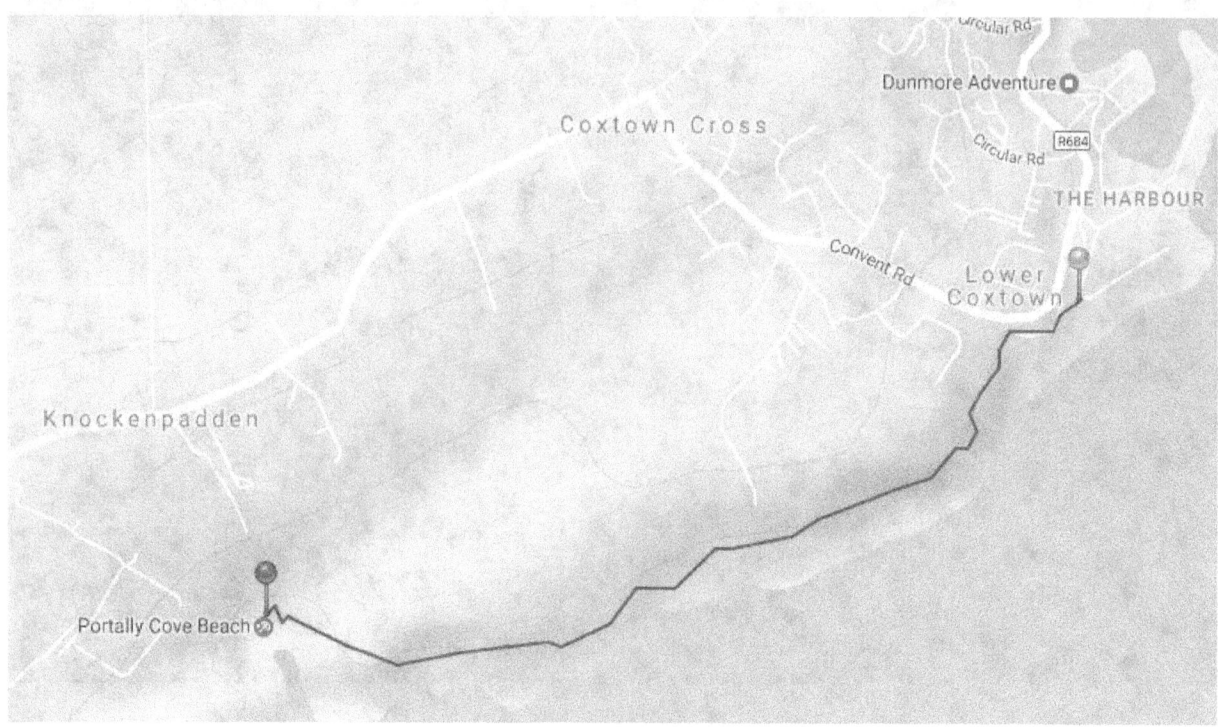

The Cliff Walk (aka Coastal Walk) between Dunmore East village and Portally Cove is approximately 30 minutes each way. The trail is well defined and set back from the cliff face for the most part. Making the approach to Portally Cove the terrain dips and the descent to the cove is completed by a number of steep steps (1-2 feet in height).

Although the walk is not looped, many people choose to walk uphill from the cove and return to the village by walking along the roadside.

Opposite (Top): The beginning of the Cliff Walk in Lower Coxtown.

Opposite (Bottom) : The remains of a rusted structure. Evidence of man's presence.

Dunmore East, Co. Waterford

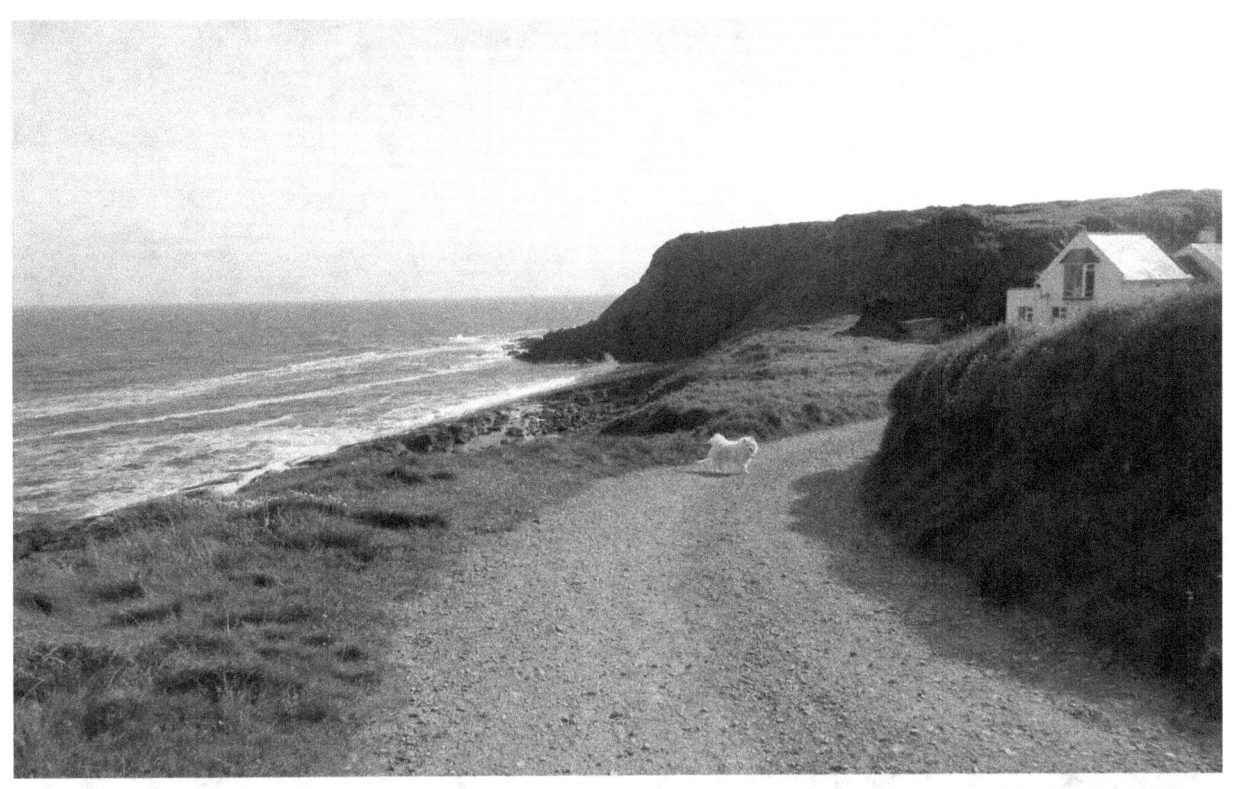

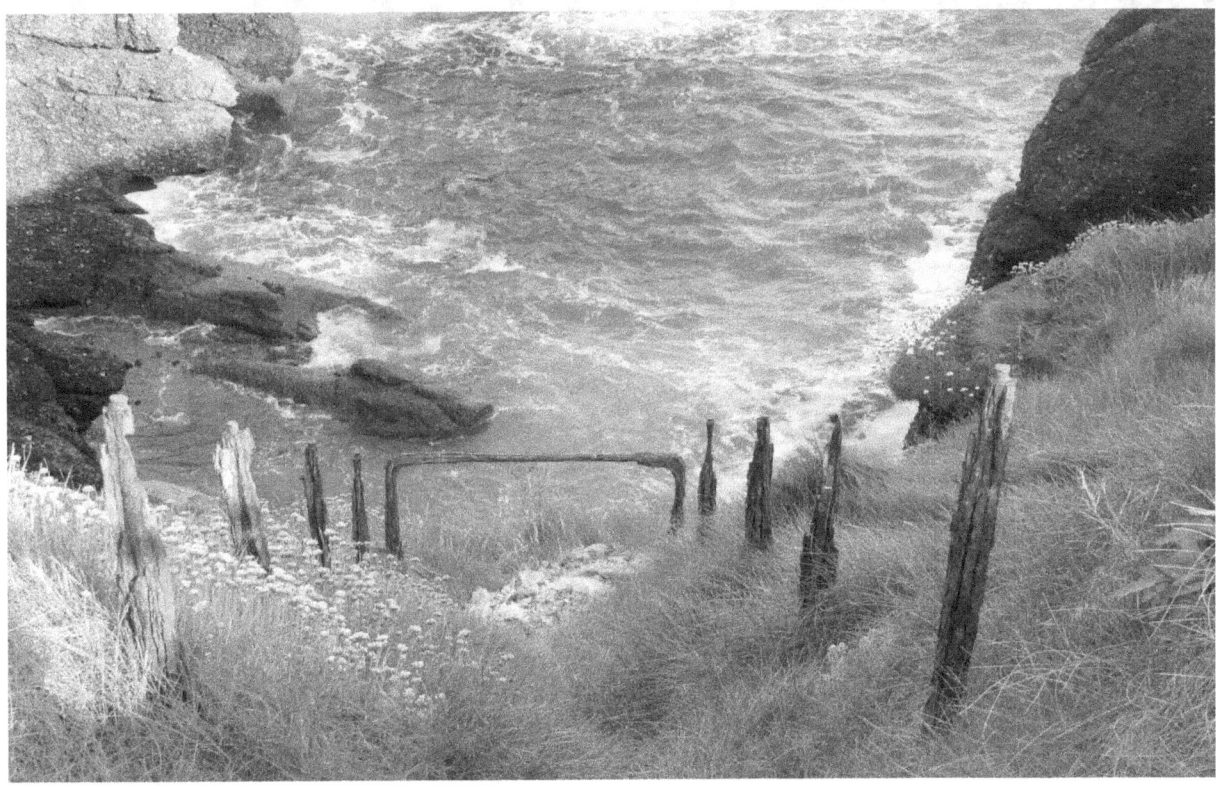

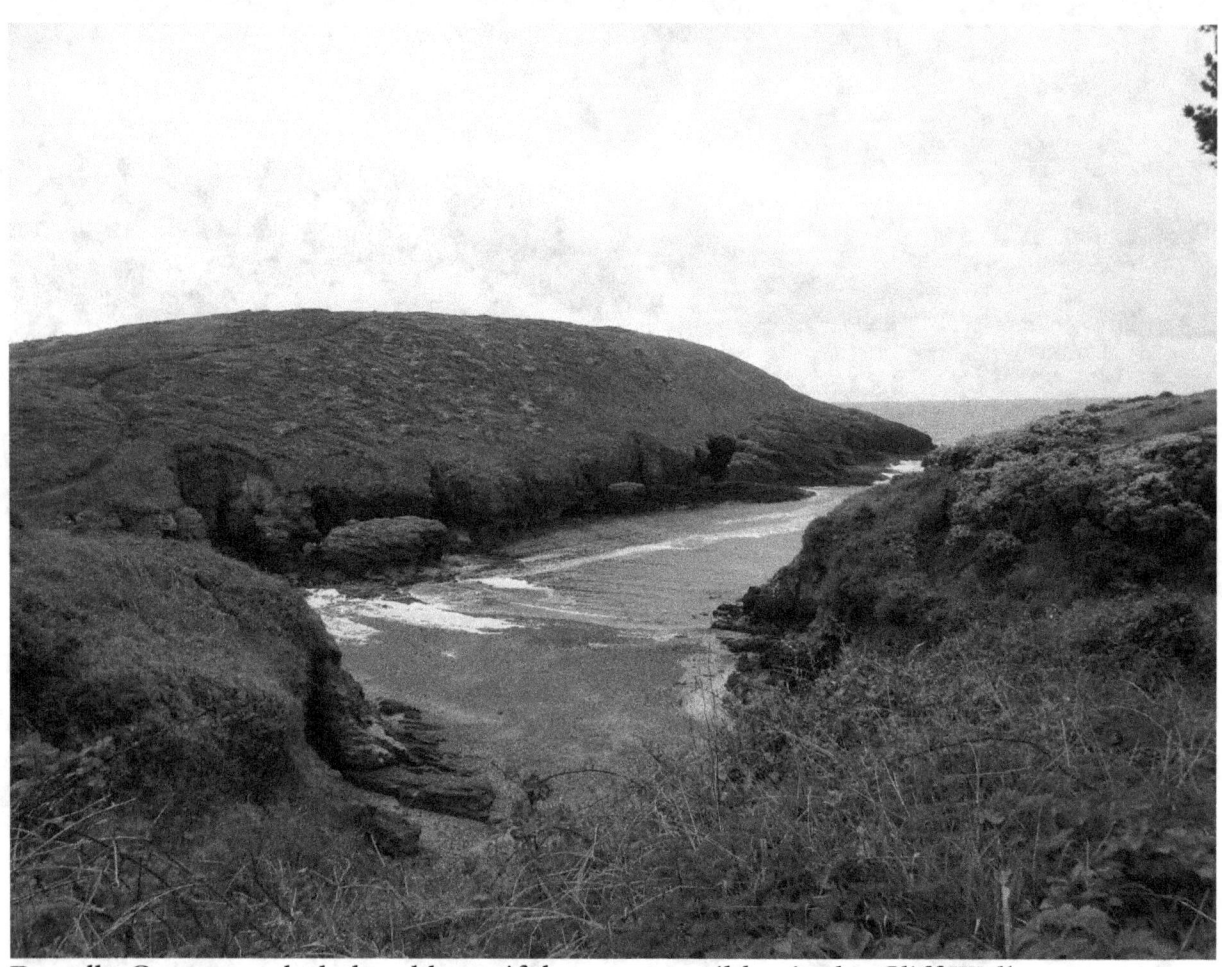

Portally Cove, a secluded and beautiful spot accessible via the Cliff Walk.

Dunmore East, Co. Waterford

Further Information

All photographs copyrighted to Emmet Tobin unless otherwise indicated.

Email : mywaterford@gmail.com

Dunmore East, Co. Waterford